Easy-Freeze

SLOW COOKER

COOKBOOK

100 Freeze-Ahead, Cook-Themselves Meals
for Every Slow Cooker

ELLA SANDERS

CASTLE POINT BOOKS
NEW YORK

ISBN 978-1-250-11660-4 (trade paperback)

Special thanks to Jennifer Calvert
Photography used under license from Shutterstock.com

Our books may be purchased in bulk for promotional, educational, or business
use. Please contact your local bookseller or the Macmillan Corporate and
Premium Sales Department at 1-800-221-7945, extension 5442,
or by email at MacmillanSpecialMarkets@macmillan.com.

First Edition: September 2018

10 9 8 7 6 5 4 3 2 1

Contents

Introduction

SLOW COOKERS ARE ONE OF THE BEST INVENTIONS FOR SAVING
time and money in the kitchen: Tough cuts of meat, which are often
less expensive, become deliciously tender when cooked for hours at a
lower temperature. As sauces simmer, flavors fuse in a way they just
can't in the oven. And you can come home after a long day to a complete
hot-and-ready meal.

But preparing that meal before you leave in the morning can be a real
headache. That's where the *Easy-Freeze Slow Cooker Cookbook* comes in.
This cookbook contains 100 simple and delicious recipes that you can make
in advance—often in under 10 minutes—and then just thaw and pour into your
slow cooker before moving on to more important things.

Some of the recipes, like Turkey Chili and Hearty Beef Lasagna, are full
and filling meals. Others, like Honey Garlic Chicken and Boneless Barbecue
Ribs, let you get the main dish out of the way while making space for the
sides. Side dishes like Balsamic Brussels Sprouts with Bacon keep the oven
clear for baking. Recipes like Fajita Chicken and Sloppy Joes prove that you
don't have to save your slow cooker for cold winter nights. In fact, why not
use it to make Red Velvet Cupcakes for your child's classroom?

All of these recipes are designed to be prepared and frozen so they're
ready when you are. But they also make great "dump dinners"—follow the
recipe but skip the freezer bag, "dumping" everything into the slow cooker the
day you want to have it. With two ways to make the most of these recipes,
you'll never run out of ideas or time. Take back your busy days by letting your
slow cooker do the work for you!

WHAT YOU'LL NEED

You'll want to have a few things on hand when preparing and cooking your freezer meals:

- Good quality 1-gallon freezer bags with white labels
- Black permanent marker
- Cooking spray
- Meat thermometer
- Slow cooker liners (optional)

TIPS AND TRICKS FOR EASY-FREEZE SLOW COOKING

Read over these tips and tricks before you get started so you can make the most of your meals:

Prepping Tips

- Label your freezer bag with the name of the recipe, the date you prepared it, and the cooking time. You can also include specific serving day ingredients and directions so that you don't have to reach for the recipe after you've prepped.
- If a piece of meat doesn't fit in a 1-gallon freezer bag, cut it into two or three pieces.
- Make sure all ingredients are cool before adding them to a freezer bag. (You don't want to melt the plastic!)
- You can use already frozen meats, vegetables, and fruits to save time and money.
- Slow cooking allows all the flavors to marry, so don't worry too much about ingredient placement in the freezer bag.
- If you're cooking for just one or two people, divide the prepared recipe into quart-size freezer bags rather than a single 1-gallon bag and use a smaller slow cooker.

Cooking Tips

- Chicken thighs are generally more forgiving, and some say more flavorful, than chicken breasts. If you're using chicken breasts, check for doneness a little earlier than the recipe calls for.

- Searing beef or pork roasts isn't necessary, but it caramelizes the outside of the meat and creates a deeper, more complex flavor.

- Some recipes call for an ingredient or two that are saved for serving day because they cook at a different rate than the others. Usually they are ingredients you're likely to have on hand anyway. And when they're not, you might be fine without them if you want to "dump and go."

- Potatoes may turn dark or become grainy if frozen raw, so recipes that use them always call for blanching them (see "How to Blanch Potatoes," page 5).

- Most of these recipes are based on using a 5- or 6-quart slow cooker, though many can still work in smaller or larger appliances. (Slow cookers work best when two-thirds full.)
- Different slow cooker brands and sizes can affect cook times, so check on your recipes periodically when you're starting out to get a sense of how your slow cooker works.

SAFETY FIRST

The recipes in this book follow USDA safety guidelines by asking you to thaw your meat overnight *in the refrigerator* before putting it in the slow cooker. (Thawing meat at room temperature for a long period of time can allow harmful bacteria to collect.) If you want to skip the thawing step, just make sure you add an hour or two to your cooking time and keep a meat thermometer handy. Your proteins need to reach the temperatures in the chart below before serving.

PRODUCT	MINIMUM INTERNAL TEMPERATURE
Beef, Pork, Veal & Lamb	145°F (62.8°C)
Ground Meats	160°F (71.1°C)
Raw Ham	145°F (62.8°C)
Pre-Cooked Ham	Fresh ham: 140°F (60°C) Leftover ham: 165°F (73.9°C)
Poultry	165°F (73.9°C)
Eggs	160°F (71.1°C)
Fish & Shellfish	145°F (62.8°C)

- Most of the recipes call for cooking on low. If you're short on time, set your slow cooker to high and cook for half the time indicated for cooking on low.

- If your food is starting to look a little too damp (especially desserts), place a paper towel between the lid and the slow cooker to catch the extra moisture, or wedge a wooden spoon under the lid to release the moisture.

- Lightly spray your slow cooker with cooking spray before adding any ingredients to keep ingredients from sticking.

- Use slow cooker liners for easy cleanup. (Spray the liner with cooking spray, just like you would the insert, to ensure that nothing sticks.)

HOW TO BLANCH POTATOES

Potatoes don't do as well as other vegetables in the freezer, so you'll need to blanch them before freezing them to ensure they retain their color, texture, and flavor in the slow cooker. Come back to this section any time you see potatoes in a recipe.

1 Bring a large pot of water to a boil, using at least 1 gallon per pound of potatoes, and add 1 tablespoon of salt to the water. Boil the potatoes in batches to avoid overcrowding them.

2 While the water comes to a boil, fill a large bowl with ice and water.

3 Once the water is boiling, thoroughly rinse the potatoes and cut them per your recipe. To reduce air exposure, cut them just before boiling them.

4 Add the potatoes to the boiling water and let them cook for 3–4 minutes. (You don't want to cook the potatoes completely because they'll fall apart while slow cooking.)

5 Using a slotted spoon, transfer the potatoes to the ice water and let them stay there for an equal amount of time.

6 Allow the potatoes to dry completely before adding them to your freezer bag.

Soups
& Stews

Serves 4

Prep Time:
20 minutes

Cook Time:
6–8 hours

Homestyle Beef Stew

Beef stew is one of those dishes that warms you from the inside out—especially when allowed to simmer and soften to perfection. The natural juices of the beef combine with the vegetables, spices, and sauces in the slow cooker until it all tastes equally amazing. Keep this recipe ready to go in your freezer and you'll always have its comforts when you need them.

PREP DAY INGREDIENTS

1½ pounds chuck roast, cubed

2 cups diced carrots

1 cup cubed potato

1 cup diced onion

3 cups low-sodium beef broth

2 tablespoons brown sugar

1 teaspoon kosher salt

¼ teaspoon freshly ground black pepper

1 teaspoon Worcestershire sauce

3 tablespoons flour

1 teaspoon chopped garlic

2 teaspoons tomato paste

SERVING DAY INGREDIENTS (OPTIONAL)

2 tablespoons cornstarch

2 tablespoons cold water

PREP DIRECTIONS

Blanch the cubed potato according to the directions on page 5. In a large bowl, combine all prep day ingredients. Label a 1-gallon freezer bag, place it in another large bowl, and pour in the stew mixture. Squeeze the remaining air out of the bag and seal it. Lay the bag flat to freeze.

SERVING DAY DIRECTIONS

Allow the stew to thaw in the refrigerator overnight. On serving day, pour the stew mixture into the slow cooker, cover it, and let it cook on low for 6–8 hours. Change the temperature setting to high 30 minutes before serving. For a thicker stew, stir together the cornstarch and water and add it to the slow cooker when you increase the temperature.

French Onion Soup

French Onion Soup takes dump dinners to the next level with the serving day addition of melted cheese and crusty bread. Just remember to buy your bread the day before you plan to serve the soup so that it has time to dry out. If you're on a low-sodium diet or are just bothered by salty foods, use low-sodium beef broth in place of regular.

PREP DAY INGREDIENTS

3 large white onions, sliced

3 tablespoons salted butter

2 tablespoons brown sugar

2 (32-ounce) cartons beef broth

1 tablespoon Worcestershire sauce

1 clove garlic, minced

⅓ cup dry sherry

4 sprigs fresh thyme or 1 teaspoon dried thyme

1 dried bay leaf

SERVING DAY INGREDIENTS

8 slices dry French bread

¾ cup Gruyère cheese, shredded

½ cup Emmental cheese, shredded

6 tablespoons fresh Parmesan cheese

PREP DIRECTIONS

In a large pan, cook the onions, butter, and brown sugar over low heat for about 20 minutes until the onions have caramelized, then allow them to cool. In a large bowl, combine the onions with the remaining prep day ingredients. Label a 1-gallon freezer bag and pour in the soup mixture. Squeeze the remaining air out of the bag and seal it. Lay the bag flat to freeze.

SERVING DAY DIRECTIONS

Allow the soup to thaw overnight in the refrigerator. On serving day, pour the soup mixture into the slow cooker, cover it, and let it cook on low for 6 hours. When finished, remove the bay leaf and ladle the soup into individual oven-safe bowls. Top each bowl with a slice of French bread and a helping of cheeses, then place the bowls in the oven to broil for 2–3 minutes until the cheese has melted and browned.

Hearty Irish Stew

This delicious Irish Stew comes together almost effortlessly—all you have to do is slice up some veggies and you have a filling meal your family will love. If your stew looks a little dry toward the end of the cooking time, add a cup of water. Otherwise, you can just dump, cook, and serve!

PREP DAY INGREDIENTS

1½–2 pounds chuck roast, cubed

1 (14-ounce) can diced tomatoes, undrained

1 (8-ounce) can tomato sauce

2 cups sliced carrots

1 cup sliced celery

1 cup diced onion

¾ cup pearl barley, rinsed and drained

5 cups beef broth

1 teaspoon kosher salt

½ teaspoon freshly ground black pepper

½ teaspoon sage

½ teaspoon thyme

1 dried bay leaf

PREP DIRECTIONS

Combine all ingredients in a large bowl. Label a 1-gallon freezer bag, place it in another large bowl, and pour in the stew mixture. Squeeze the remaining air out of the bag and seal it. Lay the bag flat to freeze.

SERVING DAY DIRECTIONS

Allow the stew to thaw overnight in the refrigerator. On serving day, pour the stew mixture into the slow cooker, cover, and let it cook on low for about 8 hours. Remove the bay leaf before serving.

Stuffed Pepper Soup

What's even easier and more satisfying than stuffed bell peppers? Stuffed Pepper Soup, which packs all that flavor into a spoonful of liquid comfort. For a healthier version, use lean ground beef, low-sodium beef broth, and a quinoa mix instead of white rice. Serve this soup with a sprinkling of cheddar cheese and a dollop of sour cream.

PREP DAY INGREDIENTS

2 pounds ground beef

1 cup diced green bell pepper

2 (15-ounce) cans diced tomatoes, undrained

1 (15-ounce) can of tomato sauce

1 (32-ounce) carton beef broth

1 cup water

1 small onion, diced

2 tablespoons brown sugar

3-4 cloves of garlic, minced

2 teaspoons kosher salt

1 teaspoon freshly ground black pepper

SERVING DAY INGREDIENTS

4 cups cooked white or brown rice

PREP DIRECTIONS

In a large pan, brown the beef over medium-high heat, then drain it and allow it to cool. Combine all prep day ingredients (including the beef) in a large bowl. Label a 1-gallon freezer bag, place it in another large bowl, and pour in the soup mixture. Squeeze the remaining air out of the bag and seal it. Lay the bag flat to freeze.

SERVING DAY DIRECTIONS

Allow the soup to thaw overnight in the refrigerator. On serving day, pour the soup mixture into the slow cooker, cover it, and let it cook on low for 6-8 hours. About 30 minutes before serving, stir in the rice, cover, and continue cooking.

Beef Chili

You usually reach for hearty stews when you need to warm up, but this Beef Chili is as perfect for sunny summer barbecues as it is for wintry nights. And once you brown the meat, your work is pretty much done, making this an easy dish to whip up for a get-together.

PREP DAY INGREDIENTS

1½ pounds ground beef

1 medium onion, diced

3 garlic cloves, minced

1 (19-ounce) can kidney beans, undrained

1 (14-ounce) can chili beans, undrained

1 (28-ounce) can diced tomatoes, undrained

1 (5½-ounce) can tomato paste

1 tablespoon chili powder

2 teaspoons cumin

½ teaspoon paprika

Freshly ground black pepper, to taste

PREP DIRECTIONS

In a large pan, brown the beef over medium-high heat. Add the onions and cook for 2-3 minutes more until they are translucent. Drain the mixture and let it cool. Combine all ingredients (including the beef and onions) in a large bowl. Label a 1-gallon freezer bag, place it in another large bowl, and pour in the chili mixture. Squeeze the remaining air out of the bag and seal it. Lay the bag flat to freeze.

SERVING DAY DIRECTIONS

Allow the chili to thaw overnight in the refrigerator. On serving day, pour the chili mixture into the slow cooker, cover it, and let it cook on low for 3-5 hours.

Creamy White Chicken Chili

Serves 4

Prep Time:
15 minutes

Cook Time:
8¼ hours

This rich White Chicken Chili recipe hits the spot with a creamy consistency and a little kick. Top it off with delicious additions like diced avocado, green onions, shredded cheese, sour cream, or a crumble of tortilla chips. If you're looking to lighten things up, just substitute in reduced-fat and low-sodium options and replace the heavy cream with half and half.

PREP DAY INGREDIENTS

1 pound boneless, skinless chicken breasts

1 yellow onion, diced

2 cloves garlic, minced

24 ounces chicken broth

2 (15-ounce) cans great northern beans, drained and rinsed

2 (4-ounce) cans diced green chiles

1 (15-ounce) can whole-kernel corn, drained

1 teaspoon kosher salt

½ teaspoon freshly ground black pepper

1 teaspoon cumin

¾ teaspoon oregano

½ teaspoon chili powder

¼ teaspoon cayenne pepper

¼ cup chopped fresh cilantro

SERVING DAY INGREDIENTS

4 ounces cream cheese, softened

¼ cup heavy cream

PREP DIRECTIONS

Combine all prep day ingredients in a large bowl. Label a 1-gallon freezer bag, place it in another large bowl, and pour in the chili mixture. Squeeze the remaining air out of the bag and seal it. Lay the bag flat to freeze.

SERVING DAY DIRECTIONS

Allow the chili to thaw overnight in the refrigerator. On serving day, pour the chili mixture into the slow cooker, cover it, and let cook on low for 8 hours. When you're almost ready to serve, remove the chicken to a cutting board or large mixing bowl, shred it, and return it to the cooker. Stir in the cream cheese and heavy cream, re-cover, and cook on high for 15 more minutes.

Sausage and Lentil Soup

Full of protein and savory flavor, Sausage and Lentil Soup is the perfect dish to serve with a fresh crust of bread on a cool day. And it tastes just as good—if not better—as a leftover, so it's also a great recipe for a couple who know they won't have time to cook during the week.

PREP DAY INGREDIENTS

12-14 ounces kielbasa sausage, sliced

1 small onion, diced

2 cups brown lentils

2 medium carrots, diced

1 medium celery rib, diced

3 cloves garlic, minced

1 (15-ounce) can diced tomatoes, undrained

½ teaspoon Italian seasoning

1 (32-ounce) carton beef stock

PREP DIRECTIONS

In a large pan, brown the sausage over medium heat. Add the onions and cook for 2-3 minutes more until they are translucent. Drain the mixture and let it cool. Combine all prep day ingredients (including the sausage and onions) in a large bowl. Label a 1-gallon freezer bag, place it in another large bowl, and pour in the soup mixture. Squeeze the remaining air out of the bag and seal it. Lay the bag flat to freeze.

SERVING DAY DIRECTIONS

Allow the soup to thaw overnight in the refrigerator. On serving day, pour the soup mixture into the slow cooker, cover it, and let it cook on low for 8-9 hours.

Traditional Chicken Noodle Soup

Serves 5

Prep Time:
15 minutes

Cook Time:
6½–7½ hours

When cold and flu season hits, what's the first thing you reach for? A bowl of the ultimate sick-day comfort food: chicken noodle soup. Of course, it'll taste just as good when you're well. An unexpected splash of lemon juice brightens up this savory soup. Don't shy away from this recipe if you're cooking for one or two—you definitely won't mind having leftovers!

PREP DAY INGREDIENTS

1½ pounds boneless, skinless chicken breasts or thighs

5 medium carrots, peeled and chopped

1 medium yellow onion, finely chopped

4 medium celery stalks, chopped

3-5 cloves garlic, minced

3 tablespoons extra virgin olive oil

6 cups low-sodium chicken broth

1 cup water

¾ teaspoon dried thyme

½ teaspoon dried rosemary, crushed

½ teaspoon dried sage

¼ teaspoon celery seed, finely crushed

2 dried bay leaves

Kosher salt and freshly ground black pepper, to taste

SERVING DAY INGREDIENTS

2 cups uncooked wide egg noodles

¼ cup chopped fresh parsley

1 tablespoon fresh lemon juice

PREP DIRECTIONS

Combine all prep day ingredients in a large bowl. Label a 1-gallon freezer bag, place it in another large bowl, and pour in the soup mixture. Squeeze the remaining air out of the bag and seal it. Lay the bag flat to freeze.

SERVING DAY DIRECTIONS

Allow the soup to thaw overnight in the refrigerator. On serving day, pour the mixture into the slow cooker, cover it, and cook on low for 6-7 hours. Toward the end of the cooking time, remove and dice the chicken. Add the egg noodles and parsley to the slow cooker, re-cover, and cook for 20-30 minutes more. Stir the chicken back into the soup and add the lemon juice before serving.

Chicken Tortilla Soup

Give Taco Tuesday a twist with this scrumptious chicken soup! The recipe calls for topping it with cheese and tortilla strips, but don't be afraid to add jalapeños, sour cream, or avocado to the mix. Finish it off with a splash of lime to balance out the savory flavor.

PREP DAY INGREDIENTS

1 pound boneless, skinless chicken breasts

1 (15-ounce) can sweet whole-kernel corn, drained

1 (15-ounce) can diced tomatoes, drained

5 cups chicken stock

¾ cup chopped onion

¾ cup chopped green bell pepper

1 serrano pepper, minced

2 cloves garlic, minced

¼ teaspoon chili powder

1 teaspoon kosher salt

¾ teaspoon freshly ground black pepper

SERVING DAY INGREDIENTS

½ teaspoon kosher salt

¼ teaspoon freshly ground black pepper

Shredded Monterey Jack cheese

Tortilla strips

PREP DIRECTIONS

Combine all prep day ingredients in a large bowl. Label a 1-gallon freezer bag, place it in another large bowl, and pour in the soup mixture. Squeeze the remaining air out of the bag and seal it. Lay the bag flat to freeze.

SERVING DAY DIRECTIONS

Allow the soup to thaw overnight in the refrigerator. On serving day, pour the mixture into the slow cooker, cover it, and cook on low for about 8 hours. Toward the end of the cooking time, remove and shred the chicken. Season it with salt and pepper before returning it to the slow cooker and stirring it in. Serve the soup topped with cheese and tortilla strips.

Black Bean Soup

Black Bean Soup—though flavorful on its own—leaves plenty of room for fresh toppings. Set the table with bowls of shredded cheese, diced tomato and avocado, and sour cream, then let your family members make it their own!

Serves 8

Prep Time:
10 minutes

Cook Time:
8 hours

PREP DAY INGREDIENTS

1 tablespoon extra virgin olive oil

1 medium yellow onion, chopped

1 medium red bell pepper, chopped

4 cloves garlic, minced

3 (15-ounce) cans black beans, drained and rinsed

8 cups chicken or vegetable broth

Kosher salt and freshly ground black pepper, to taste

SERVING DAY INGREDIENTS

½ cup chopped fresh cilantro

Juice of 1 lime

PREP DIRECTIONS

Add the chopped onion and peppers to a large pan and sauté them over medium heat until the onion is translucent. Stir in the garlic until it becomes fragrant, about 1 minute. Allow the mixture to cool, then combine it with the rest of the prep day ingredients in a large bowl. Label a 1-gallon freezer bag, place it in another large bowl, and pour in the soup mixture. Squeeze the remaining air out of the bag and seal it. Lay the bag flat to freeze.

SERVING DAY DIRECTIONS

Allow the soup to thaw overnight in the refrigerator. On serving day, pour the soup mixture into the slow cooker, cover it, and cook on low for about 8 hours. Stir in the cilantro and lime juice about 15 minutes before serving.

Creamy Chicken and Potato Soup

Chicken, potatoes, garlic, and cheese: this tasty dish combines all your favorite foods in one bowl. Because it makes a large batch, it would be perfect for potlucks or as an appetizer at family gatherings. Just put out bowls of toppings, such as crumbled bacon, shredded cheddar cheese, sour cream, and chives, so that guests can help themselves.

PREP DAY INGREDIENTS

5 cups peeled and cubed russet potatoes

1½ pounds boneless, skinless chicken breasts

1 cup yellow onion, chopped

¾ cups sliced carrots

½ cup chopped celery

3 cloves garlic, minced

2½ teaspoons kosher salt

1 teaspoon freshly ground black pepper

1 teaspoon dried thyme

2 dried bay leaves

4 cups chicken broth

SERVING DAY INGREDIENTS

1½ cups heavy cream

¼ cup all-purpose flour

Kosher salt and freshly ground black pepper, to taste

PREP DIRECTIONS

Blanch the potatoes according to the directions on page 5. Combine all prep day ingredients in a large bowl. Label a 1-gallon freezer bag, place it in another large bowl, and pour in the soup mixture. Squeeze the remaining air out of the bag and seal it. Lay the bag flat to freeze.

SERVING DAY DIRECTIONS

Allow the soup to thaw overnight in the refrigerator. On serving day, pour the mixture into the slow cooker, cover it, and cook on low for about 8 hours. Toward the end of the cooking time, remove and shred the chicken. In a small bowl, whisk together the heavy cream and flour. Slowly pour the mixture into the slow cooker, stir in the chicken, re-cover, and cook for 30 more minutes. Season with salt and pepper, to taste, before serving.

Ham and Lentil Stew

Serves 8

Prep Time:
10 minutes

Cook Time:
7-9 hours

If you're looking for a way to use up leftover ham, look no further than this simple stew. Serve it up with fresh buttery biscuits for a meal that will hit the spot on a busy weekday.

PREP DAY INGREDIENTS

1 (16-ounce) package dried lentils

4 cups water

3 cups diced cooked ham

2 cups chopped celery

2 cups chopped carrot

2 (10-ounce) cans chicken broth

PREP DIRECTIONS

Combine all ingredients in a large bowl. Label a 1-gallon freezer bag, place it in another large bowl, and pour in the stew mixture. Squeeze the remaining air out of the bag and seal it. Lay the bag flat to freeze.

SERVING DAY DIRECTIONS

Allow the stew to thaw overnight in the refrigerator. On serving day, pour the mixture into the slow cooker, cover it, and cook on low for 7-9 hours.

Chicken Chili Verde

Serves 6-8

Prep Time:
5 minutes

Cook Time:
4-6 hours

When you're used to traditional beef chili, this Chicken Chili Verde is a bright change of pace. Serve it topped with sour cream and cilantro, over rice, or even wrapped up in tortillas with a splash of lime juice, a little shredded cheese, and some fresh avocado.

PREP DAY INGREDIENTS

1 pound boneless, skinless chicken thighs

1 pound boneless, skinless chicken breasts

1 (12-ounce) jar salsa verde

1 (4-ounce) can fire-roasted green chiles

2 (15-ounce) cans great northern beans, drained and rinsed

½ teaspoon ground cumin

½ teaspoon dried oregano

Kosher salt and freshly ground black pepper, to taste

PREP DIRECTIONS

Combine all ingredients in a large bowl. Label a 1-gallon freezer bag, place it in another large bowl, and pour in the chili. Squeeze the remaining air out of the bag and seal it. Lay the bag flat to freeze.

SERVING DAY DIRECTIONS

Allow the chili to thaw overnight in the refrigerator. On serving day, pour the mixture into the slow cooker, cover it, and cook on low for 4-6 hours. Toward the end of the cooking time, remove and shred the chicken. Stir it back into the chili before serving.

Loaded Baked Potato Soup

Is using a can of soup to make more soup cheating? No—it's smart! This simple, effortless soup tastes anything but and will soon become one of your go-to recipes. Top things off with more bacon crumbles, shredded cheddar cheese, green onions, or even jalapeños for a little extra flavor.

PREP DAY INGREDIENTS

½ pound bacon

5 pounds potatoes, peeled and diced

1 medium onion, diced

1 (8-ounce) container sour cream

1 (14.5-ounce) can chicken broth

1 (10.75-ounce) can cream of chicken soup

PREP DIRECTIONS

In a large pan, fry the bacon over medium heat, turning often, until crisp. Allow it to cool, then crumble it. Blanch the potatoes according to the directions on page 5. Combine all ingredients in a large bowl. Label a 1-gallon freezer bag, place it in another large bowl, and pour in the soup mixture. Squeeze the remaining air out of the bag and seal it. Lay the bag flat to freeze.

SERVING DAY DIRECTIONS

Allow the soup to thaw overnight in the refrigerator. On serving day, pour the mixture into the slow cooker, cover it, and cook on low for 8-10 hours.

Turkey Chili

If you're trying to reduce the amount of red meat in your diet, you'll definitely want to give this healthy and flavorful Turkey Chili a try. You'll never miss the ground beef! Serve it topped with shredded cheese, green onions, and a dollop of sour cream, plus a side of crusty bread or cornbread.

Serves 8

Prep Time:
20 minutes

Cook Time:
8 hours

PREP DAY INGREDIENTS

1 tablespoon olive oil

1 medium white onion, chopped

4 cloves garlic, minced

1 medium red bell pepper, chopped

1 pound ground turkey

1½ teaspoons kosher salt

½ teaspoon cumin

1 teaspoon oregano

1 (1.25-ounce) package chili seasoning

1 tablespoon tomato paste

1 cup chicken broth

1 tablespoon brown rice flour

1 (25-ounce) jar plain pasta sauce

1 (15-ounce) can black beans, rinsed

1 (15-ounce) can pinto beans, rinsed

1 (15-ounce) can kidney beans, rinsed

PREP DIRECTIONS

Heat the olive oil in a large skillet over medium heat. Add the onion, garlic, and pepper and cook for 3–5 minutes until soft. Add the ground turkey and cook, stirring and breaking it up, until browned. Stir in the salt, spices, and seasoning, then stir in the tomato paste, broth, and flour. Let it cool, then combine the mixture with the remaining ingredients in a large bowl. Label a 1-gallon freezer bag, place it in another large bowl, and pour in the chili mixture. Squeeze the remaining air out of the bag and seal it. Lay the bag flat to freeze.

SERVING DAY DIRECTIONS

Allow the chili to thaw overnight in the refrigerator. On serving day, pour the mixture into the slow cooker, cover it, and cook on low for about 8 hours.

Split Pea Soup with Turkey Bacon

This Split Pea Soup is chock full of flavor and veggies! Turkey bacon keeps it light, but you can always sub in the real thing if you miss it. This is also a great recipe for using up leftover ham—just dice it up and throw it into the freezer bag instead of the turkey bacon.

PREP DAY INGREDIENTS

2 cups diced uncured turkey bacon

1 pound dry split peas

1 large yellow onion, diced

1 cup chopped celery

2 cups chopped carrot

3 cloves of garlic, minced

½ teaspoon thyme

2 dried bay leaves

1 (32-ounce) carton chicken broth

2 cups water

PREP DIRECTIONS

Combine all ingredients in a large bowl. Label a 1-gallon freezer bag, place it in another large bowl, and pour in the soup mixture. Squeeze the remaining air out of the bag and seal it. Lay the bag flat to freeze.

SERVING DAY DIRECTIONS

Allow the soup to thaw overnight in the refrigerator. On serving day, pour the mixture into the slow cooker, cover it, and cook on low for 7–8 hours. Remove the bay leaves before serving.

Sausage and Shrimp Creole

This hearty gumbo packs some punch with Creole seasoning and will hit the spot when served over rice. Seafood cooks up quickly, so the trick is to add it toward the end of your cooking time. If you're not a fan of shrimp, add 2 pounds of chicken breasts to your freezer bag instead, and shred them before serving.

PREP DAY INGREDIENTS

1 pound Andouille sausage, sliced

1 cup chopped onion

½ cup flour

1 (32-ounce) carton chicken broth

2 tablespoons Creole seasoning

1 tablespoon garlic powder

3 dried bay leaves

SERVING DAY INGREDIENTS

2 pounds cooked and frozen shrimp

PREP DIRECTIONS

Combine all prep day ingredients in a large bowl. Label a 1-gallon freezer bag, place it in another large bowl, and pour in the mixture. Squeeze the remaining air out of the bag and seal it. Lay the bag flat to freeze.

SERVING DAY DIRECTIONS

Allow the mixture to thaw overnight in the refrigerator. On serving day, pour the contents of the freezer bag into the slow cooker, cover it, and cook on low for about 6 hours. About 30 minutes before serving, remove the bay leaves and add the shrimp, re-cover, and cook until the shrimp are firm and pink.

Seafood Stew

Serves 8

Prep Time:
15 minutes

Cook Time:
4½–5 hours

If you're a seafood lover, this is the recipe for you! Seafood Stew is packed with whitefish, shrimp, clams, and crabmeat. Because it cooks so quickly, you'll need to add all of that seafood on serving day toward the end of your cook time. But being able to pull the prepared base from your freezer means this is still an almost effortless meal.

PREP DAY INGREDIENTS

2 cups chopped onion

1 cup chopped celery

5 cloves garlic, minced

1 (28-ounce) can diced tomatoes, undrained

1 (8-ounce) bottle clam juice

1 (6-ounce) can tomato paste

½ cup dry white wine or water

1 tablespoon red wine vinegar

1 tablespoon olive oil

2½ teaspoons dried Italian seasoning

¼ teaspoon sugar

¼ teaspoon crushed red pepper flakes

1 dried bay leaf

SERVING DAY INGREDIENTS

1 pound firm-fleshed whitefish, cut into 1-inch pieces

¾ pound shelled, deveined, uncooked medium shrimp, tails removed

1 (6.5-ounce) can chopped clams with juice, undrained

1 (6-ounce) can crabmeat, drained

¼ cup chopped fresh parsley

PREP DIRECTIONS

Combine all prep day ingredients in a large bowl. Label a 1-gallon freezer bag, place it in another large bowl, and pour in the mixture. Squeeze the remaining air out of the bag and seal it. Lay the bag flat to freeze.

SERVING DAY DIRECTIONS

Allow the stew to thaw overnight in the refrigerator. On serving day, pour the mixture into the slow cooker, cover it, and cook on high for 4 hours. Stir the serving day ingredients into the stew, re-cover, and cook for an additional 30–45 minutes, until a fork can easily flake the fish. Discard the bay leaf, stir in the parsley, and serve.

Veggie Stew

Trying to incorporate healthier meals into your diet? With filling and flavorful Veggie Stew, you'll never miss the meat. Top it off with some basil or even a little shredded cheese, and you'll have a happy family on your hands.

Serves 4

Prep Time:
15 minutes

Cook Time:
7–8 hours

PREP DAY INGREDIENTS

3 small carrots, diced

3 small potatoes, diced

1 small yellow onion, diced

3 cloves garlic, minced

1 (15-ounce) can red beans, undrained

2 cups trout beans, par-cooked

1 (15-ounce) can sweet whole-kernel corn

1 (28-ounce) can diced tomatoes, undrained

2 tablespoons kosher salt

½ teaspoon ground cumin

1 teaspoon Aleppo pepper

2 tablespoons red bell pepper flakes

¼ teaspoon freshly ground black pepper

1 teaspoon ground chili powder

2 cups water

PREP DIRECTIONS

Blanch the potatoes according to the directions on page 5. Combine all ingredients in a large bowl. Label a 1-gallon freezer bag, place it in another large bowl, and pour in the soup mixture. Squeeze the remaining air out of the bag and seal it. Lay the bag flat to freeze.

SERVING DAY DIRECTIONS

Allow the soup to thaw overnight in the refrigerator. On serving day, pour the mixture into the slow cooker, cover it, and cook on low for 7–8 hours.

Minestrone Soup

If you crave a certain Italian-style restaurant's minestrone soup, this recipe will hit the spot. Speed things up by using frozen veggies instead of fresh.

PREP DAY INGREDIENTS

2 (14.5-ounce) cans diced tomatoes, undrained

2 tablespoons tomato paste

¼ cup sun-dried tomato pesto

1 (15-ounce) can red kidney beans, drained and rinsed

1 (15-ounce) can great northern beans, drained and rinsed

1 Parmesan rind

4 cups vegetable stock

2 cups water

1 cup diced carrots

1¼ cup diced celery

1½ cup diced white onion

4-5 cloves garlic, minced

1 teaspoon dried oregano

1 sprig fresh rosemary or ½ teaspoon dried rosemary

2 dried bay leaves

Kosher salt and freshly ground pepper, to taste

SERVING DAY INGREDIENTS

1½ cups diced zucchini

1½ cups macaroni or shell pasta

1 cup green beans (fresh or thawed)

2½ cups baby spinach, chopped

Shredded Parmesan or Romano cheese, for serving

PREP DIRECTIONS

Combine all prep day ingredients in a large bowl. Label a 1-gallon freezer bag, place it in another large bowl, and pour in the soup mixture. Squeeze the remaining air out of the bag and seal it. Lay the bag flat to freeze.

SERVING DAY DIRECTIONS

Allow the soup to thaw overnight in the refrigerator. On serving day, pour the mixture into the slow cooker, cover it, and cook on low for 7-8 hours. Once the beans and vegetables are cooked through and tender, add the zucchini and pasta and cook on high for an additional 20-25 minutes until the pasta is tender. Then add the green beans and spinach and cook for 5 minutes more. Serve individual portions topped with shredded cheese.

Spiced Butternut Squash Soup

Serves 6–8

Prep Time:
10 minutes

Cook Time:
7–8 hours

Cinnamon and curry powder spice up this simple soup while green apples balance things out. You'll blend everything when it's done cooking to get that wonderfully creamy consistency, so don't worry about chopping up the fruits and veggies too finely.

PREP DAY INGREDIENTS

2-2¼ pounds butternut squash, chopped

1 large yellow onion, chopped

2 medium granny smith apples, chopped

2 medium carrots, chopped

2 tablespoons light brown sugar

1 tablespoon kosher salt

1 teaspoon freshly ground black pepper

2 dried bay leaves

1-2 tablespoons curry powder (mild or hot)

¼ teaspoon cinnamon powder

1 teaspoon minced fresh ginger

1 tablespoon minced garlic

2 cups chicken or vegetable broth

SERVING DAY INGREDIENTS

½ cup heavy cream

PREP DIRECTIONS

Combine all prep day ingredients in a large bowl. Label a 1-gallon freezer bag, place it in another large bowl, and pour in the soup mixture. Squeeze the remaining air out of the bag and seal it. Lay the bag flat to freeze.

SERVING DAY DIRECTIONS

Allow the soup to thaw overnight in the refrigerator. On serving day, pour the soup mixture into the slow cooker, cover it, and cook on low for 7-8 hours. Remove the bay leaves. Blend the soup using an immersion blender or standing blender, then stir in the cream, and serve.

Sweet Potato and Cauliflower Soup

If you have trouble getting your daily serving of veggies, Sweet Potato and Cauliflower Soup is a must-try. It's a healthy dish masquerading as a comfort food! And if it still feels a little *too* green for your taste, go ahead and top it off with some bacon and cheddar cheese.

PREP DAY INGREDIENTS

2 pounds fresh cauliflower, roughly chopped

2 pounds sweet potatoes, peeled and cubed

1 (32-ounce) carton chicken or vegetable broth

1 large onion, diced

5 cloves garlic, peeled

4 stalks green onion, chopped

1 teaspoon dried thyme

1 teaspoon paprika

Red pepper flakes, to taste

Kosher salt, to taste

SERVING DAY INGREDIENTS

2 cups 2% milk

2 ounces cream cheese

PREP DIRECTIONS

Blanch the potatoes according to the directions on page 5. Combine all prep day ingredients in a large bowl. Label a 1-gallon freezer bag, place it in another large bowl, and pour in the soup mixture. Squeeze the remaining air out of the bag and seal it. Lay the bag flat to freeze.

SERVING DAY DIRECTIONS

Allow the soup to thaw overnight in the refrigerator. On serving day, pour the mixture into the slow cooker, cover it, and cook on low for 8-9 hours. Blend the soup using an immersion blender or standing blender. Stir in the milk and cream cheese and continue to blend until smooth, then serve.

Side Dishes

Cheesy Quinoa with Mushrooms and Peppers

They don't call quinoa a superfood for nothing—this hearty grain is a complete protein unto itself. That makes it the perfect base for just about any vegetarian dish. This recipe uses cheese and seasonings to turn quinoa into an Italian-inspired meal.

PREP DAY INGREDIENTS

1 (32-ounce) carton vegetable broth

2 cups uncooked quinoa

2 medium green onions, chopped

½ medium red pepper, diced

8 ounces sliced mushrooms

4 ounces cream cheese

1 tablespoon minced garlic

1 teaspoon Italian seasoning

Kosher salt and freshly ground black pepper, to taste

SERVING DAY INGREDIENTS

1 cup shredded Parmesan or Italian-blend cheese

PREP DIRECTIONS

Label a 1-gallon freezer bag and add all prep day ingredients to it. Squeeze the remaining air out of the bag and seal it. Lay the bag flat to freeze.

SERVING DAY DIRECTIONS

Allow the bag to thaw overnight in the refrigerator. On serving day, pour the mixture into the slow cooker, cover it, and cook on low for 4–5 hours. Stir to combine. Sprinkle the cheese over the quinoa mixture, re-cover, and let the cheese melt for 15 minutes before serving.

Honeyed Peas and Carrots

Honey, butter, and garlic turn a boring bag of frozen peas and carrots into a rich dish you'll reach for again and again. While slow cooking helps the flavors meld, keeping the peas separate until just before serving ensures that they're tender without being mushy.

PREP DAY INGREDIENTS

1 pound carrots, sliced

1 large onion, chopped

¼ cup water

¼ cup honey

4 tablespoons unsalted butter, cubed

4 garlic cloves, minced

1 teaspoon kosher salt

1 teaspoon dried marjoram

⅛ teaspoon white pepper

SERVING DAY INGREDIENTS

1 (16-ounce) package frozen peas

PREP DIRECTIONS

Combine all prep day ingredients in a large bowl. Label a 1-gallon freezer bag, place it in another large bowl, and pour in the carrot mixture. Squeeze the remaining air out of the bag and seal it. Lay the bag flat to freeze.

SERVING DAY DIRECTIONS

Allow the carrots to thaw overnight in the refrigerator. On serving day, pour the mixture into the slow cooker, cover it, and cook on low for about 5 hours. Stir in the frozen peas, re-cover, and continue to cook for another 15–25 minutes until the peas are tender.

Brown Sugar Green Beans

Serves 12

Prep Time:
5 minutes

Cook Time:
2–3 hours

Is there anything that a little brown sugar can't make better? This quick recipe turns basic green beans into a side dish your family will ask for by name. The sweetness of these greens makes them a great addition to pork chops or barbecue ribs.

PREP DAY INGREDIENTS

3 pounds French-style green beans

1 stick unsalted butter, melted

½ cup packed brown sugar

1½ teaspoons garlic salt

¾ teaspoon reduced-sodium soy sauce

PREP DIRECTIONS

Combine all ingredients in a large bowl. Label a 1-gallon freezer bag, place it in another large bowl, and pour in the mixture. Squeeze the remaining air out of the bag and seal it. Lay the bag flat to freeze.

SERVING DAY DIRECTIONS

Allow the green beans to thaw overnight in the refrigerator. On serving day, pour the mixture into the slow cooker, cover it, and cook on low for 2–3 hours.

Glazed Carrots

Finding new and exciting ways to whip up vegetables is half the battle in eating healthy, and this Glazed Carrots recipe is a winner. The slow cooker allows the carrots to simmer all day in butter, brown sugar, and spices so you get flavorful veggies without any fuss.

Serves 6

Prep Time:
10 minutes

Cook Time:
6–8 hours

PREP DAY INGREDIENTS

2 pounds carrots, sliced

½ cup peach preserves

1 stick butter, melted

¼ cup packed brown sugar

1 teaspoon vanilla extract

½ teaspoon ground cinnamon

¼ teaspoon salt

⅛ teaspoon ground nutmeg

2 tablespoons cornstarch

2 tablespoons water

PREP DIRECTIONS

Combine all ingredients in a large bowl. Label a 1-gallon freezer bag, place it in another large bowl, and pour in the mixture. Squeeze the remaining air out of the bag and seal it. Lay the bag flat to freeze.

SERVING DAY DIRECTIONS

Allow the carrots to thaw overnight in the refrigerator. On serving day, pour the mixture into the slow cooker, cover it, and cook on low for 6–8 hours, until the carrots are tender.

Serves 12

Prep Time:
15 minutes

Cook Time:
5-6 hours

Maple-Pecan Sweet Potatoes

Maple Pecan Sweet Potatoes is a dish packed with healthful superfoods but still yummy enough to convert sweet-potato skeptics and picky kids alike. This sweet and easy side dish makes 12 servings—perfect for a party or family gathering!

PREP DAY INGREDIENTS

4 pounds sweet potatoes, sliced ½-inch thick

½ cup coarsely chopped pecans

½ cup packed light brown sugar

½ cup coarsely chopped dried cherries

½ cup maple syrup

¼ cup apple cider or juice

¼ teaspoon kosher salt

SERVING DAY INGREDIENTS

¼ cup coarsely chopped pecans

PREP DIRECTIONS

Blanch the sweet potatoes according to the directions on page 5. Combine all prep day ingredients in a large bowl. Label a 1-gallon freezer bag, place it in another large bowl, and pour in the mixture. Squeeze the remaining air out of the bag and seal it. Lay the bag flat to freeze.

SERVING DAY DIRECTIONS

Allow the sweet potatoes to thaw overnight in the refrigerator. On serving day, pour the mixture into the slow cooker, cover it, and cook on low for 5-6 hours. Top with chopped pecans before serving.

Candied Sweet Potatoes

Serves 6–8

Prep Time:
15 minutes

Cook Time:
4 hours

Candied Sweet Potatoes are the perfect complement to big meals, not only because they're delicious but also because making them in the slow cooker frees up the oven and stove for other things. If you like a little spice, add ½ teaspoon each of cinnamon, nutmeg, and ginger to the mix before freezing.

PREP DAY INGREDIENTS

4 pounds sweet potatoes, peeled and sliced ½-inch thick

1 cup granulated sugar

1 cup packed brown sugar

2 teaspoons vanilla extract

¼ teaspoon kosher salt

4 tablespoons unsalted butter, melted

SERVING DAY INGREDIENTS

2 tablespoons cornstarch

PREP DIRECTIONS

Blanch the sweet potatoes according to the directions on page 5, then add them to a labeled 1-gallon freezer bag. In a small bowl, whisk together the sugars, then whisk in the vanilla, salt, and butter. Pour the mixture over the potatoes, squeeze the remaining air out of the bag, and seal it. Lay the bag flat to freeze.

SERVING DAY DIRECTIONS

Allow the sweet potatoes to thaw overnight in the refrigerator. On serving day, pour the mixture into the slow cooker, cover it, and cook on low for about 4 hours, until the potatoes are tender. Move the potatoes to a serving dish using a slotted spoon. Pour the remaining liquid into a medium saucepan, whisk in the cornstarch, then bring the mixture to a boil over medium heat. Continue cooking until the sauce has thickened, about 1–2 minutes, then pour it over the potatoes.

Easy Rice Pilaf

If freezable slow cooker recipes aren't easy enough, Easy Rice Pilaf uses a can of cream of mushroom soup to bring big flavor with none of the work. Brighten things up with a sprinkling of fresh parsley before serving with any of your favorite mains.

PREP DAY INGREDIENTS

¾ cup wild rice, uncooked

½ cup long-cooking brown rice, uncooked

½ pound portabella mushrooms, sliced 1-inch thick

1 (10.75-ounce) can cream of mushroom with roasted garlic soup

1½ cups water

⅛ teaspoon freshly ground black pepper

PREP DIRECTIONS

Combine all ingredients in a large bowl. Label a 1-gallon freezer bag, place it in another large bowl, and pour in the mixture. Squeeze the remaining air out of the bag and seal it. Lay the bag flat to freeze.

SERVING DAY DIRECTIONS

Allow the mixture to thaw overnight in the refrigerator. On serving day, pour it into the slow cooker, cover it, and cook on low for 6-7 hours.

Balsamic Root Vegetables

With sweet potatoes, dried cranberries, and brown sugar, this simple side couldn't be better suited to crisp fall days—especially Thanksgiving. Top it with a little parsley for color, or a crumble of cooked bacon for a hint of savory flavor.

PREP DAY INGREDIENTS

1½ pounds sweet potatoes, peeled cut into chunks

1 pound parsnips, peeled and cut into chunks

1 pound carrots, peeled and cut into chunks

1 large red onion, coarsely chopped

¾ cup sweetened dried cranberries

1 tablespoon light brown sugar

3 tablespoons olive oil

2 tablespoons balsamic vinegar

1 teaspoon kosher salt

½ teaspoon freshly ground pepper

PREP DIRECTIONS

Blanch the potatoes according to the directions on page 5. Label a 1-gallon freezer bag and add the sweet potatoes, parsnips, carrots, onion, and cranberries to it. In a small bowl, whisk together the remaining prep day ingredients. Pour the mixture into the freezer bag, squeeze the remaining air out of the bag, and seal it. Lay the bag flat to freeze.

SERVING DAY DIRECTIONS

Allow the vegetable mixture to thaw overnight in the refrigerator. On serving day, pour the mixture into the slow cooker, cover it, and cook on low for 8-9 hours, until the vegetables are tender.

Creamy Potatoes and Peppers

Serves 4

Prep Time:
10 minutes

Cook Time:
6–8 hours

A little mustard and a can of cream of chicken soup are all you need to transform potatoes into a side dish your family will love—and one that's easy enough to make any day of the week. Just let everything simmer all day while you check other things off your to-do list.

PREP DAY INGREDIENTS

6 medium potatoes, peeled and sliced

1 (10.75-ounce) can cream of chicken soup

3 tablespoons Dijon mustard

1 medium onion, sliced

1 medium green pepper, sliced

PREP DIRECTIONS

Blanch the potatoes according to the directions on page 5. Combine the potatoes, soup, and mustard in a large bowl. Place a labeled 1-gallon freezer bag in another large bowl, add the sliced onion and pepper, then pour in the potato mixture. Squeeze the remaining air out of the bag and seal it. Lay the bag flat to freeze.

SERVING DAY DIRECTIONS

Allow the mixture to thaw overnight in the refrigerator. On serving day, pour it into the slow cooker, cover it, and cook on low for 6–8 hours.

Barbecue Baked Beans

Serves 6-8

Prep Time:
5 minutes

Cook Time:
8-9 hours

With just a handful of ingredients and a day of slow cooking, Barbecue Baked Beans taste gourmet. Use your go-to barbecue sauce, or spice things up with any of the intriguing varieties at your local store. Then serve the beans alongside pulled pork, hamburgers, or barbecued ribs.

PREP DAY INGREDIENTS

1 (16-ounce) package dried pinto beans

3 cups water

1 medium onion, chopped

1 (18-ounce) bottle barbecue sauce

¼ cup molasses

¼ teaspoon freshly ground black pepper

PREP DIRECTIONS

Combine all ingredients in a large bowl. Label a 1-gallon freezer bag, place it in another large bowl, and pour in the mixture. Squeeze the remaining air out of the bag and seal it. Lay the bag flat to freeze.

SERVING DAY DIRECTIONS

Allow the mixture to thaw overnight in the refrigerator. On serving day, pour it into the slow cooker, cover it, and cook on low for 8-9 hours.

Wild Rice with Peppers

Wild rice is full of protein and fiber, plus it's good for both your heart and your digestive system. Toss in some onions and peppers, and you have a healthy and flavorful side for any dish.

PREP DAY INGREDIENTS

1 cup wild rice, uncooked

½ cup sliced mushrooms

½ cup diced onions

½ cup diced red peppers

1 tablespoon olive oil

1 teaspoon kosher salt

¼ teaspoon freshly ground black pepper

2½ cups chicken broth

PREP DIRECTIONS

Combine all ingredients in a large bowl. Label a 1-gallon freezer bag, place it in another large bowl, and pour in the mixture. Squeeze the remaining air out of the bag and seal it. Lay the bag flat to freeze.

SERVING DAY DIRECTIONS

Allow the rice mixture to thaw overnight in the refrigerator. On serving day, pour it into the slow cooker, cover it, and cook on low for 5-6 hours or until the rice has absorbed the liquid.

Caribbean Black Beans

Serves 8

Prep Time:
10 minutes

Cook Time:
5-6 hours

Sure, you could add some boring black beans straight from the can to your burrito bowl. But nothing beats beans that have spent hours simmering with bright and flavorful veggies and spices. So why settle?

PREP DAY INGREDIENTS

2 (15-ounce) cans black beans, drained and rinsed

½ cup water

1 cup chopped green bell pepper

½ cup chopped onion

1 teaspoon ground cumin

½ teaspoon kosher salt

½ teaspoon garlic powder

1 (2-ounce) jar diced pimientos, drained

PREP DIRECTIONS

Combine all ingredients in a large bowl. Label a 1-gallon freezer bag, place it in another large bowl, and pour in the mixture. Squeeze the remaining air out of the bag and seal it. Lay the bag flat to freeze.

SERVING DAY DIRECTIONS

Allow the beans to thaw overnight in the refrigerator. On serving day, pour the mixture into the slow cooker, cover it, and cook on low for 5-6 hours.

Classic Cornbread

When you're serving up comfort food like chili or roasted chicken, boring biscuits just won't hit the spot. That's when you reach into your freezer for this buttery cornbread. If you like a little kick, stir 1 teaspoon of chili powder into the batter before freezing it.

PREP DAY INGREDIENTS

1½ cups cornmeal

1½ cups all-purpose flour

2 tablespoons baking powder

1 teaspoon kosher salt

2 cups buttermilk

2 large eggs

SERVING DAY INGREDIENTS

2 tablespoons unsalted butter

PREP DIRECTIONS

Combine all prep day ingredients in a large bowl to create a batter. Label a 1-gallon freezer bag, place it in another large bowl, and pour in the mixture. Squeeze the remaining air out of the bag and seal it. Lay the bag flat to freeze.

SERVING DAY DIRECTIONS

Allow the batter to thaw in the refrigerator overnight. On serving day, add the butter to the slow cooker, allow it to melt, and coat the bottom of the cooker with it. Pour the batter into the slow cooker so that it spreads evenly over the bottom, cover it, and cook on high for 2 hours. Let the cornbread cool before serving.

Zesty Cranberry Sauce

Serves 8

Prep Time:
10 minutes

Cook Time:
8 hours

Zesty Cranberry Sauce is as perfect a companion served warm with holiday dinners as it is served cold in summertime. As a bonus, this fruity side dish fills the whole house with a heavenly smell while it simmers. Serve it chunky or blend it to the consistency you like.

PREP DAY INGREDIENTS

4 medium apples, peeled and chopped

1 (12-ounce) bag fresh cranberries

½ cup packed brown sugar

1 teaspoon grated orange peel

¼ cup orange juice

PREP DIRECTIONS

Combine all ingredients in a large bowl. Label a 1-gallon freezer bag, place it in another large bowl, and pour in the mixture. Squeeze the remaining air out of the bag and seal it. Lay the bag flat to freeze.

SERVING DAY DIRECTIONS

Allow the sauce to thaw overnight in the refrigerator. On serving day, pour the mixture into the slow cooker, cover it, and cook on low for about 8 hours.

Garlic-Ranch Potatoes

Once you give these simple but delicious Garlic Ranch Potatoes a try, they'll become a dinnertime staple at your house. They're also great for potlucks and picnics, especially since you can pull them out of the freezer on short notice.

PREP DAY INGREDIENTS

3 pounds red potatoes, washed and quartered

2 tablespoons salted butter

2 tablespoons olive oil

1 (1-ounce) packet ranch seasoning

1 tablespoon chopped chives

1 tablespoon minced garlic

Kosher salt and freshly ground pepper, to taste

PREP DIRECTIONS

Blanch the potatoes according to the directions on page 5. Combine all ingredients in a large bowl. Label a 1-gallon freezer bag, place it in another large bowl, and pour in the mixture. Squeeze the remaining air out of the bag and seal it. Lay the bag flat to freeze.

SERVING DAY DIRECTIONS

Allow the potatoes to thaw overnight in the refrigerator. On serving day, pour the mixture into the slow cooker, cover it, and cook on high for 3-4 hours. Stir the potatoes after 1 hour and start checking for doneness after 2 hours. They should be fork tender before serving.

Orange-Glazed Carrots

Orange juice and brown sugar bring out the natural sweetness of baby carrots for a side dish even picky eaters will love. And because this recipe uses ingredients you probably have on hand, it's an easy one to check off when you're prepping a bunch of recipes at once.

PREP DAY INGREDIENTS

2 pounds baby carrots

½ cup packed brown sugar

½ cup orange juice

3 tablespoons unsalted butter

¾ teaspoon cinnamon

¼ teaspoon nutmeg

SERVING DAY INGREDIENTS

2 tablespoons cornstarch

¼ cup water

PREP DIRECTIONS

Combine all prep day ingredients in a large bowl. Label a 1-gallon freezer bag, place it in another large bowl, and pour in the carrot mixture. Squeeze the remaining air out of the bag and seal it. Lay the bag flat to freeze.

SERVING DAY DIRECTIONS

Allow the carrots to thaw overnight in the refrigerator. On serving day, pour them into the slow cooker, cover it, and cook on low for 3-4 hours until the carrots are tender-crisp. When they're done, remove them using a slotted spoon, then add the remaining juices to a small saucepan and bring them to a boil. Stir in the cornstarch and water until the glaze has thickened. Pour the glaze over the carrots before serving.

Black-Eyed Peas and Ham

Freeze-ahead meals are a great way to use up leftovers so that you're not eating the same things for a week after a big meal. This recipe uses cooked ham to add protein and savory flavor to black-eyed peas and greens.

Serves 12

Prep Time: 10 minutes

Cook Time: 9 hours

PREP DAY INGREDIENTS

2 cups dried black-eyed peas, sorted and rinsed

4 cups chicken broth

2 cups diced cooked ham

1 cup water

½ teaspoon kosher salt

¼ teaspoon ground red (cayenne) pepper

3 cloves garlic, finely chopped

½ cup chopped carrots

2 sprigs fresh thyme

1 cup chopped onion

1 jalapeño pepper, seeded and chopped

SERVING DAY INGREDIENTS

5 cups torn escarole or kale

PREP DIRECTIONS

Combine all prep day ingredients in a large bowl. Label a 1-gallon freezer bag, place it in another large bowl, and pour in the mixture. Squeeze the remaining air out of the bag and seal it. Lay the bag flat to freeze.

SERVING DAY DIRECTIONS

Allow the mixture to thaw overnight in the refrigerator. On serving day, pour it into the slow cooker, cover it, and cook on low for about 8 hours or until the peas are tender. Stir in the escarole or kale, re-cover, and cook for 1 more hour until the greens are tender and wilted.

Balsamic Brussels Sprouts with Bacon

Serves 6

Prep Time:
10 minutes

Cook Time:
3-4 hours

A balsamic reduction and bacon bring out the best in these Brussels sprouts! Making the balsamic reduction on serving day won't take too much time, but you can just as easily make it on prep day. Just freeze it in a small, freezer-safe container or bag alongside the Brussels sprouts, allow it to thaw, and add it to the slow cooker for the last 15-20 minutes of cook time.

PREP DAY INGREDIENTS

½ pound bacon

2 pounds Brussels sprouts, trimmed and halved

2 tablespoons olive oil

2 tablespoons unsalted butter, cubed

Kosher salt and freshly ground black pepper, to taste

SERVING DAY INGREDIENTS

½ cup balsamic vinegar

2 tablespoons brown sugar, packed

¼ cup crumbled blue cheese (optional)

PREP DIRECTIONS

In a large pan, fry the bacon over medium heat, turning often, until crisp. Allow it to cool, then crumble it. Combine all prep day ingredients in a large bowl. Label a 1-gallon freezer bag, place it in another large bowl, and pour in the mixture. Squeeze the remaining air out of the bag and seal it. Lay the bag flat to freeze.

SERVING DAY DIRECTIONS

Allow the mixture to thaw overnight in the refrigerator. On serving day, pour the mixture into the slow cooker, cover it, and cook on low for 3-4 hours. While the Brussels sprouts cook, bring the balsamic vinegar and brown sugar to a slight boil in a small saucepan over medium heat. Allow it to reduce by half (6-8 minutes), then set it aside to cool. When the Brussels sprouts have finished cooking, serve with a drizzle of the balsamic reduction and a sprinkling of blue cheese.

Barbecue-Style Green Beans

With just a little effort ahead of time, amazingly tasty Barbecue-Style Green Beans can be as weeknight friendly as the plain, old freezer variety. But thanks to a few extra ingredients, they'll take any family meal up a notch.

PREP DAY INGREDIENTS

1 pound bacon

¼ cup chopped onions

¾ cup ketchup

½ cup brown sugar

3 teaspoons Worcestershire sauce

¾ teaspoon kosher salt

4 cups green beans

PREP DIRECTIONS

In a large pan, fry the bacon over medium heat, turning often, until crisp. Set it aside. While the bacon cools, add the onions to the pan with the bacon drippings and sauté until translucent, 2-3 minutes. Stir in the crumbled bacon, ketchup, sugar, Worcestershire sauce, and salt. Lightly combine the sauce with the green beans in a large bowl. Label a 1-gallon freezer bag, place it in another large bowl, and pour in the mixture. Squeeze the remaining air out of the bag and seal it. Lay the bag flat to freeze.

SERVING DAY DIRECTIONS

Allow the green beans to thaw overnight in the refrigerator. On serving day, pour the mixture into the slow cooker, cover it, and cook on low for 6-8 hours.

Baked Beans with Bacon

Whether you serve them at a picnic or at a family dinner, baked beans are one of those classic side dishes that make everyone smile. If you want to make a vegetarian version, you can simply omit the bacon or swap it out for green or red peppers.

PREP DAY INGREDIENTS

2 (15-ounce) cans great northern beans, drained and rinsed

½ cup barbecue sauce

½ cup ketchup

1 cup chopped onions

4 slices uncooked bacon, diced

PREP DIRECTIONS

Combine all ingredients in a large bowl. Label a 1-gallon freezer bag, place it in another large bowl, and pour in the mixture. Squeeze the remaining air out of the bag and seal it. Lay the bag flat to freeze.

SERVING DAY DIRECTIONS

Allow the mixture to thaw overnight in the refrigerator. On serving day, pour it into the slow cooker, cover it, and cook on low for about 6 hours.

Main Dishes

Cilantro-Lime Chicken with Corn Salsa

With a recipe this easy, you're out of excuses for serving the same old slow cooker meals. Spice up an ordinary night with deliciously citrusy chicken. If you're watching your weight, forgo the tortillas in favor of lettuce and maybe go light on the shredded cheese. If not, turn it into a burrito bowl over rice and add toppings to your heart's content! (Did someone say avocado?)

PREP DAY INGREDIENTS

2 boneless, skinless chicken breasts

1 bunch fresh cilantro, chopped

1 medium red onion, chopped

1 (15-ounce) can black beans, drained and rinsed

2 cups whole-kernel corn

2 teaspoons minced garlic

1 teaspoon ground cumin

Juice of 2 limes

SERVING DAY INGREDIENTS (OPTIONAL)

4-6 tortillas or lettuce leaves

Shredded cheese, to taste

PREP DIRECTIONS

Combine all prep day ingredients in a large bowl. Label a 1-gallon freezer bag, place it in another large bowl, and pour in the mixture. Squeeze the remaining air out of the bag and seal it. Lay the bag flat to freeze.

SERVING DAY DIRECTIONS

Allow the chicken mixture to thaw overnight in the refrigerator. On serving day, pour it into the slow cooker, cover it, and cook on low for about 8 hours. Using two forks, shred the chicken and stir the mixture well. Serve topped with cheese on tortillas or lettuce.

Teriyaki Chicken with Pineapple

With just five ingredients and a few minutes of your time, you can put a delicious meal on the table any night of the week. The pineapple-infused sauce that simmers around the chicken is amazing over both rice and steamed veggies.

PREP DAY INGREDIENTS

2 pounds boneless, skinless chicken thighs

1 (20-ounce) can pineapple chunks, with liquid

½ cup soy sauce

¼ cup rice wine vinegar

¼ cup brown sugar

PREP DIRECTIONS

Combine all ingredients in a large bowl. Label a 1-gallon freezer bag, place it in another large bowl, and pour in the mixture. Squeeze the remaining air out of the bag and seal it. Lay the bag flat to freeze.

SERVING DAY DIRECTIONS

Allow the chicken to thaw overnight in the refrigerator. On serving day, pour the mixture into the slow cooker, cover it, and cook on low for about 8 hours.

Ginger-Peach Chicken

Serves 6

Prep Time:
10 minutes

Cook Time:
7–8 hours

The best thing about using a slow cooker is how it allows all the flavors of a dish to marry. In Ginger Peach Chicken, a bit of red onion brings the bite while juicy peaches perfectly balance out the ginger and soy sauce. The end result is a dish you can't resist!

PREP DAY INGREDIENTS

2 pounds boneless, skinless chicken thighs

1 (12-ounce) bag frozen peach slices

1 cup chicken broth

½ medium red onion, sliced

2 tablespoons brown sugar

2 tablespoons soy sauce

1 tablespoon freshly grated ginger

2 teaspoons ground coriander

PREP DIRECTIONS

Combine all ingredients in a large bowl. Label a 1-gallon freezer bag, place it in another large bowl, and pour in the mixture. Squeeze the remaining air out of the bag and seal it. Lay the bag flat to freeze.

SERVING DAY DIRECTIONS

Allow the chicken to thaw overnight in the refrigerator. On serving day, pour the mixture into the slow cooker, cover it, and cook on low for 7–8 hours.

Sweet Fire Chicken

If you like the take-out version of Sweet Fire Chicken, then you'll love this healthier version! The sweetness of pineapple and peppers and the heat of chili sauce fuse perfectly over a few hours in the slow cooker.

Serves 4

Prep Time:
10 minutes

Cook Time:
4½–5½ hours

PREP DAY INGREDIENTS

2 teaspoons minced garlic

1-2 teaspoons crushed red pepper flakes

⅔ cup sugar

1 cup water

2 tablespoons sweet red chili sauce

½ teaspoon kosher salt

3-4 boneless, skinless chicken breasts, diced

1 large red bell pepper, chopped

1 (20-ounce) can pineapple chunks, drained

SERVING DAY INGREDIENTS

4 tablespoons cold water

3 tablespoons cornstarch

PREP DIRECTIONS

Whisk together the first 6 prep day ingredients in a large bowl. Stir in the chicken, pepper, and pineapple until combined. Label a 1-gallon freezer bag, place it in another large bowl, and pour in the mixture. Squeeze the remaining air out of the bag and seal it. Lay the bag flat to freeze.

SERVING DAY DIRECTIONS

Allow the chicken to thaw overnight in the refrigerator. On serving day, pour the mixture into the slow cooker, cover it, and cook on low for 4-5 hours. Before serving, whisk together the cold water and cornstarch in a small bowl. Stir the slurry into the slow cooker, re-cover, and let everything cook on high for another 30 minutes.

Creamy Lemon Chicken

For this dish, you're going to sear in some flavor before letting it simmer. If you're feeling fancy, place the slices of lemony chicken over pasta in cream sauce and top it with a sprinkling of Parmesan cheese. Or simply serve the chicken alongside roasted reds and your favorite veggies.

PREP DAY INGREDIENTS

6 tablespoons unsalted butter, divided

½ teaspoon kosher salt

¼ teaspoon freshly ground black pepper

1 teaspoon Italian seasoning

5 boneless, skinless chicken breasts

Juice and zest of 2 lemons

2 cloves garlic, minced

SERVING DAY INGREDIENTS

1 cup half-and-half

1 tablespoon cornstarch

PREP DIRECTIONS

Melt 1 tablespoon of butter in a large skillet over medium-high heat. Stir in the salt, pepper, and Italian seasoning, then add the chicken. Brown the chicken for 4–6 minutes on each side. Put the chicken, lemon juice and zest, garlic, and remaining butter (sliced into pats) into a labeled 1-gallon freezer bag. Squeeze the remaining air out of the bag and seal it. Lay the bag flat to freeze.

SERVING DAY DIRECTIONS

Allow the chicken to thaw overnight in the refrigerator. On serving day, pour the mixture into the slow cooker, cover it, and cook on low for about 4 hours. Whisk together the half-and-half and cornstarch in a small bowl. Add this creamy mixture to the slow cooker, stir, re-cover, and let the chicken continue to cook for 1 more hour on high.

Fajita Chicken

Serves 4-6

Prep Time:
10 minutes

Cook Time:
4½-5½ hours

Whether you layer Fajita Chicken over lettuce or serve it on warm tortillas, you'll have an easy meal that everyone can enjoy. Set out toppings like cheese, sour cream, diced tomatoes, and avocado slices, and let everyone create their own fajita masterpiece.

PREP DAY INGREDIENTS

1½ pounds boneless, skinless chicken breast

1 medium red pepper, seeded and sliced

1 medium green pepper, seeded and sliced

1 medium onion, sliced

½ cup chicken broth

1 packet taco seasoning

1 teaspoon chili powder

½ teaspoon paprika

1 teaspoon kosher salt

PREP DIRECTIONS

Combine all ingredients in a large bowl. Label a 1-gallon freezer bag, place it in another large bowl, and pour in the mixture. Squeeze the remaining air out of the bag and seal it. Lay the bag flat to freeze.

SERVING DAY DIRECTIONS

Allow the chicken to thaw overnight in the refrigerator. On serving day, pour the mixture into the slow cooker, cover it, and cook on low for 4-5 hours. Remove the chicken from the slow cooker and shred it. Stir the chicken back into the sauce, re-cover the slow cooker, and let everything continue to cook for another 30 minutes.

Honey-Sesame Chicken

Honey Sesame Chicken is one of those better-than-take-out meals that will become a regular part of your weeknight routine. Serve it over steamed broccoli and rice, and finish it off with green onions and a sprinkling of sesame seeds.

PREP DAY INGREDIENTS

1 small onion, diced

2 cloves garlic, minced

½ cup honey

½ cup soy sauce

¼ cup ketchup

2 tablespoons vegetable oil

¼ teaspoon crushed red pepper flakes

Kosher salt and freshly ground black pepper, to taste

2 pounds boneless, skinless chicken thighs

PREP DIRECTIONS

Combine all ingredients in a large bowl. Label a 1-gallon freezer bag, place it in another large bowl, and pour in the mixture. Squeeze the remaining air out of the bag and seal it. Lay the bag flat to freeze.

SERVING DAY DIRECTIONS

Allow the chicken to thaw overnight in the refrigerator. On serving day, pour the mixture into the slow cooker, cover it, and cook on low for 3 hours and 30 minutes. Remove the chicken from the slow cooker and shred or slice it. Stir the chicken back into the sauce, re-cover, and let everything continue to cook for another 30 minutes.

Honey-Garlic Chicken

Honey Garlic Chicken tastes indulgent but is still easy on the waistline, especially if you serve it with green veggies. Finish things off with a sprinkle of sesame seeds. If you find the sauce too thin for your liking, stir in a tablespoon or two of cornstarch before serving.

PREP DAY INGREDIENTS

4 garlic cloves, minced

⅓ cup honey

½ cup ketchup

½ cup low-sodium soy sauce

½ teaspoon dried oregano

2 tablespoons fresh parsley

6 boneless, skinless chicken thighs

PREP DIRECTIONS

Combine all ingredients except the chicken in a large bowl, then add the chicken and toss it in the sauce. Label a 1-gallon freezer bag, place it in another large bowl, and pour in the mixture. Squeeze the remaining air out of the bag and seal it. Lay the bag flat to freeze.

SERVING DAY DIRECTIONS

Allow the chicken to thaw overnight in the refrigerator. On serving day, pour the mixture into the slow cooker, cover it, and cook on low for 4-5 hours.

Honeyed Chicken and Vegetables

Serves 4

Prep Time:
15 minutes

Cook Time:
7–8 hours

Does tomorrow's schedule make you think pizza's your only option? That's when you move this bag from the freezer to the fridge. Roasted red potatoes and veggies soak up sweet honey-garlic sauce right alongside succulent chicken thighs for a meal that will help you slow down during a packed day.

PREP DAY INGREDIENTS

8 bone-in, skin-on chicken thighs

1 pound baby red potatoes, halved

1 pound baby carrots

½ cup reduced-sodium soy sauce

½ cup honey

¼ cup ketchup

2 cloves garlic, minced

1 teaspoon dried basil

½ teaspoon dried oregano

¼ teaspoon crushed red pepper flakes

¼ teaspoon freshly ground black pepper

SERVING DAY INGREDIENTS

1 pound green beans, trimmed

PREP DIRECTIONS

Blanch the potatoes according to the directions on page 5. Add the chicken, potatoes, and carrots to a labeled 1-gallon freezer bag. Combine the rest of the prep day ingredients in a large bowl, then pour the mixture into the bag over the chicken. Squeeze the remaining air out of the bag and seal it. Lay the bag flat to freeze.

SERVING DAY DIRECTIONS

Allow the chicken to thaw overnight in the refrigerator. On serving day, pour the mixture into the slow cooker, cover it, and cook on low for 7–8 hours. Add the green beans to the slow cooker 30 minutes before serving, making sure to cover them in the sauce.

Barbecue Chicken Sandwiches

Serves 4-6

Prep Time:
15 minutes

Cook Time:
6½–8½ hours

Tangy barbecue chicken proves that slow cookers aren't just great for warm-you-from-the-inside winter dinners. Pile it high on your favorite kind of roll for a pulled-chicken sandwich that will make your mouth water any time of year.

PREP DAY INGREDIENTS

2 pounds boneless, skinless chicken breasts

1 cup ketchup

¼ cup molasses

¼–⅓ cup packed brown sugar

2 tablespoons seedless blackberry preserves

2½ tablespoons cider vinegar

2 teaspoons liquid smoke

1 teaspoon smoked paprika

1 teaspoon chili powder

1 teaspoon onion powder

1 teaspoon garlic powder

1 teaspoon kosher salt

½ teaspoon freshly ground black pepper

¼ teaspoon dried thyme

¼ teaspoon chipotle chili powder or cayenne pepper

SERVING DAY INGREDIENTS

1 tablespoon cornstarch

2 tablespoons water

PREP DIRECTIONS

Label a 1-gallon freezer bag and add the chicken to it. Combine the rest of the prep day ingredients in a large bowl, then pour the mixture into the bag over the chicken. Squeeze the remaining air out of the bag and seal it. Lay the bag flat to freeze.

SERVING DAY DIRECTIONS

Allow the chicken to thaw overnight in the refrigerator. On serving day, pour the mixture into the slow cooker, cover it, and cook on low for 6-8 hours. Remove the chicken from the slow cooker and shred it. In a small bowl, mix together the cornstarch and water, then stir the mixture into the sauce in the slow cooker. Stir the chicken back into the sauce, re-cover the slow cooker, and let everything continue to cook for 20-30 minutes.

Lemon-Pesto Chicken

Lemon Pesto Chicken is equally delicious over pasta, served with veggies, or even layered into a flatbread sandwich, which makes it a great go-to main dish to have on hand. Any way you make it, shave a little Parmesan cheese over the top to finish things off.

PREP DAY INGREDIENTS

1½ pounds boneless, skinless chicken breasts

1 cup chicken broth

¼ cup freshly squeezed lemon juice

½ cup jarred basil pesto

¼ teaspoon kosher salt

¼ teaspoon freshly ground black pepper

PREP DIRECTIONS

Combine all ingredients in a large bowl. Label a 1-gallon freezer bag, place it in another large bowl, and pour in the mixture. Squeeze the remaining air out of the bag and seal it. Lay the bag flat to freeze.

SERVING DAY DIRECTIONS

Allow the chicken to thaw overnight in the refrigerator. On serving day, pour the mixture into the slow cooker, cover it, and cook on low for 6-8 hours.

Sweet Teriyaki Chicken

Serves 4-6

Prep Time:
10 minutes

Cook Time:
2½–3½ hours

When you're tempted to order in, reach into the freezer for this much-better take on take-out instead. This recipe uses cornstarch to thicken up the juices left in the slow cooker. For an even tastier sauce, transfer it to a saucepan to boil on medium-high heat for about 15 minutes. Add the cornstarch slurry to the reduced sauce and let it thicken for another 1-2 minutes before serving.

PREP DAY INGREDIENTS

2 pounds boneless, skinless chicken thighs

1 cup diced yellow onion

2 cloves garlic, minced

½ cup soy sauce

½ cup honey

¼ cup rice vinegar

¼ teaspoon freshly ground black pepper

1 tablespoon grated peeled fresh ginger

SERVING DAY INGREDIENTS

¼ cup water

2 tablespoons cornstarch

PREP DIRECTIONS

Put the chicken into a labeled 1-gallon freezer bag. Combine the rest of the prep day ingredients in a large bowl, then pour the mixture into the bag over the chicken. Squeeze the remaining air out of the bag and seal it. Lay the bag flat to freeze.

SERVING DAY DIRECTIONS

Allow the chicken to thaw overnight in the refrigerator. On serving day, pour the mixture into the slow cooker, cover it, and cook on low for 2-3 hours. Remove the chicken from the slow cooker and cut it into bite-size pieces. In a small bowl, mix together the cornstarch and water, then stir the mixture into the sauce in the slow cooker. Stir the chicken back into the sauce, re-cover the slow cooker, and let everything continue to cook for another 20 minutes.

Orange-Pepper Chicken Wings

These sweet-and-spicy Asian-inspired wings would make a wonderful addition to any potluck or picnic. Finish them with a sprinkling of sesame seeds and maybe some freshly sliced scallions.

PREP DAY INGREDIENTS

8 large chicken wings (sectioned and tips removed) or drumsticks

⅓ cup honey

2 tablespoons orange juice

3 tablespoons soy sauce

1 tablespoon rice vinegar

2 tablespoons ground ginger

½ tablespoon red pepper flakes

PREP DIRECTIONS

Place the chicken in a labeled 1-gallon freezer bag. Combine the rest of the prep day ingredients in a large bowl, then pour the mixture into the bag over the chicken. Squeeze the remaining air out of the bag and seal it. Lay the bag flat to freeze.

SERVING DAY DIRECTIONS

Allow the chicken to thaw overnight in the refrigerator. On serving day, pour the mixture into the slow cooker, cover it, and cook on low for about 4 hours.

Curried Chicken

Toss rich Curried Chicken over instant brown rice for a filling meal that doesn't fill your day with cooking chores. To brighten things up, you can add frozen peas during the last 15-25 minutes of cooking time and a splash of lime juice before serving.

Serves 4

Prep Time:
15 minutes

Cook Time:
4½ hours

PREP DAY INGREDIENTS

4 medium potatoes, cubed

3 boneless, skinless chicken breasts

1 cup chopped onion

1 (8-ounce) package sliced mushrooms

1 (14-ounce) can stewed tomatoes, undrained

1 cup water

2 tablespoons curry paste

2 teaspoons minced garlic

2 teaspoons ginger

2 teaspoons turmeric

SERVING DAY INGREDIENT (OPTIONAL)

1 medium red bell pepper, diced

PREP DIRECTIONS

Blanch the potatoes according to the directions on page 5. Combine all prep day ingredients in a large bowl. Label a 1-gallon freezer bag, place it in another large bowl, and pour in the mixture. Squeeze the remaining air out of the bag and seal it. Lay the bag flat to freeze.

SERVING DAY DIRECTIONS

Allow the chicken to thaw overnight in the refrigerator. On serving day, pour the mixture into the slow cooker, cover it, and cook on low for about 3 hours. Add the diced bell pepper to the slow cooker and continue cooking for about 1 more hour. Remove the chicken from the slow cooker and cut it into bite-size pieces. Stir it back into the sauce, re-cover the slow cooker, and let everything continue to cook for another 20-30 minutes.

Chicken-Apple Sausage and Sweet Potatoes

Everything about this recipe—from the sweet potatoes to the apple juice and cinnamon—says *fall*. If you want not just the flavor of the peppers but also the color, wait until the last hour on serving day to add them to the slow cooker.

PREP DAY INGREDIENTS

4 medium sweet potatoes, peeled and cubed

1 (12-ounce) package chicken-apple sausage, sliced

½ cup sliced bell peppers

1 cup apple juice

⅔ cup brown sugar

1 teaspoon cinnamon

1 teaspoon fresh thyme leaves

1 teaspoon fresh dill leaves

Kosher salt and freshly ground pepper, to taste

PREP DIRECTIONS

Blanch the potatoes according to the directions on page 5. Combine all ingredients in a large bowl. Label a 1-gallon freezer bag, place it in another large bowl, and pour in the mixture. Squeeze the remaining air out of the bag and seal it. Lay the bag flat to freeze.

SERVING DAY DIRECTIONS

Allow the mixture to thaw overnight in the refrigerator. On serving day, pour everything into the slow cooker, cover it, and cook on low for about 6 hours.

Spicy Chicken Pasta

Spicy Chicken Pasta is the perfect blend of creamy with a kick for a mouthwatering feel *and* flavor. If you want a spicier pasta, go lighter on the cream. If you want a milder pasta, go heavier on the cream. Then serve the pasta with a salad and veggies topped with a vinegar-based dressing to balance things out.

PREP DAY INGREDIENTS

1 pound boneless, skinless chicken breast

1 tablespoon cornstarch

1 tablespoon water

2½ cups chicken broth

¼ cup hot sauce

1 (8-ounce) can tomato sauce

¼ cup brown sugar

¼ teaspoon red pepper flakes

SERVING DAY INGREDIENTS

¼–½ cup heavy cream

10 ounces uncooked pasta, such as spaghetti or linguini

PREP DIRECTIONS

Place the chicken in a labeled 1-gallon freezer bag. Whisk together the cornstarch and water in a small bowl. Combine the rest of the prep day ingredients, including the cornstarch slurry, in a large bowl, then pour the mixture into the bag over the chicken. Squeeze the remaining air out of the bag and seal it. Lay the bag flat to freeze.

SERVING DAY DIRECTIONS

Allow the chicken to thaw overnight in the refrigerator. On serving day, pour the mixture into the slow cooker, cover it, and cook on low for 6–8 hours. Remove the chicken from the slow cooker and cut it into bite-size pieces. Turn the slow cooker up to high and stir in the chicken, cream, and pasta. Allow everything to cook for up to an additional 45 minutes, stirring occasionally, until the pasta is al dente.

Turkey Enchilada Bowl

Turkey, veggies, and quinoa make this a meal you can feel good about serving to your family. And having a table full of their favorite toppings—like sour cream, shredded cheese, green onions, and avocado—will make them feel good about it, too.

PREP DAY INGREDIENTS

1 tablespoon olive oil

½ cup diced onion

½ cup diced red bell pepper

1 pound ground turkey

1½ cups uncooked quinoa, rinsed

1 (15-ounce) can black beans, drained and rinsed

1 cup whole-kernel corn

1 (10-ounce) can diced tomatoes and green chiles, undrained

½ cup salsa

1 teaspoon minced garlic

1 cup water

1 (19-ounce) can red enchilada sauce

1 tablespoon chili powder

1 teaspoon cumin

PREP DIRECTIONS

Heat the olive oil in a large skillet over medium heat. Add the onion and red pepper and cook for 3-5 minutes or until soft. Add the ground turkey and cook, stirring and breaking it up, until browned. Let cool, then combine the mixture with the remaining ingredients in a large bowl. Label a 1-gallon freezer bag, place it in another large bowl, and pour in the turkey mixture. Squeeze the remaining air out of the bag and seal it. Lay the bag flat to freeze.

SERVING DAY DIRECTIONS

Allow the enchilada mixture to thaw overnight in the refrigerator. On serving day, pour the mixture into the slow cooker, cover it, and cook on low for about 6 hours.

Turkey-Stuffed Peppers

Serves 6

Prep Time:
10 minutes

Cook Time:
6 hours

Ground turkey lightens up this already wholesome dish, which would be equally delicious with lean ground beef. The recipe calls for using fresh peppers on serving day, but you can absolutely fill and freeze the peppers on prep day if you have room in your freezer.

PREP DAY INGREDIENTS

1 tablespoon olive oil

½ cup chopped onion

1 teaspoon minced garlic

1 pound lean ground turkey

1 (14-ounce) can diced tomatoes, undrained

1 cup whole-kernel corn

1 cup brown rice, cooked

2 tablespoons Worcestershire sauce

1 teaspoon kosher salt

1 teaspoon freshly ground pepper

1 cup shredded Mexican-blend cheese

SERVING DAY INGREDIENTS

6 large bell peppers, any color

PREP DIRECTIONS

Heat the olive oil in a large skillet over medium heat. Add the onion and garlic and cook for 2-3 minutes until fragrant. Add the ground turkey and cook, stirring and breaking it up, until browned. Let cool, then combine the mixture with the remaining prep day ingredients in a large bowl. Label a 1-gallon freezer bag, place it in another large bowl, and pour in the turkey mixture. Squeeze the remaining air out of the bag and seal it. Lay the bag flat to freeze.

SERVING DAY DIRECTIONS

Allow the turkey mixture to thaw overnight in the refrigerator. On serving day, slice the tops off the peppers and remove their cores and seeds. Fill each pepper with a serving of the turkey mixture, place them in the slow cooker, cover it, and cook on low for about 6 hours.

Serves 4-6

Prep Time:
10 minutes

Cook Time:
6½-8½ hours

Pot-Pie Style Chicken

Few things are more comforting than chicken pot pie. Keep the peas and carrots bright and tender (rather than colorless and mushy) by adding them toward the end of the cooking time. While your slow cooker does the brunt of the work, you can just put some refrigerated biscuits in the oven to complete the dish.

PREP DAY INGREDIENTS

4 medium potatoes, peeled and diced

4 boneless, skinless chicken breasts

2 (10.75-ounce) cans condensed cream of chicken soup

1 chicken bouillon cube

SERVING DAY INGREDIENTS

1 (16-ounce) package frozen peas and carrots

PREP DIRECTIONS

Blanch the potatoes according to the directions on page 5. Combine all prep day ingredients in a large bowl. Label a 1-gallon freezer bag, place it in another large bowl, and pour in the mixture. Squeeze the remaining air out of the bag and seal it. Lay the bag flat to freeze.

SERVING DAY DIRECTIONS

Allow the chicken to thaw overnight in the refrigerator. On serving day, pour the mixture into the slow cooker, cover it, and cook on low for 6-8 hours. About 1 hour before serving, stir in the frozen peas and carrots. Just before serving, remove the chicken from the slow cooker and shred it. Stir the chicken back into the sauce, re-cover the slow cooker, and let everything continue to cook for another 20-30 minutes.

Sweet Pork with Apples and Pears

Serves 6

Prep Time:
10 minutes

Cook Time:
6–8 hours

Some flavors are made for each other, and savory pork paired with sweet fruit might just top the list. With a few additions like onion, brown sugar, and mustard, you'll have a dish that tastes gourmet in no time at all. Even better: every member of the family will love it!

PREP DAY INGREDIENTS

3 pounds cubed pork shoulder

3 medium apples, sliced

2 medium pears, sliced

1 medium onion, sliced

1½ cups brown sugar

3 tablespoons mustard

1½ cups apple juice

½ cup vinegar

SERVING DAY INGREDIENTS

2½ cups water

PREP DIRECTIONS

Combine all prep day ingredients in a large bowl. Label a 1-gallon freezer bag, place it in another large bowl, and pour in the mixture. Squeeze the remaining air out of the bag and seal it. Lay the bag flat to freeze.

SERVING DAY DIRECTIONS

Allow the pork mixture to thaw overnight in the refrigerator. On serving day, pour 2½ cups water and the contents of the freezer bag into the slow cooker, cover it, and cook on low for 6–8 hours.

Balsamic Pork Roast

Balsamic Pork Roast simmers in its sweet and tangy sauce for 8 to 10 hours, making it a great choice for the end of an extra-long day at the office. If you don't want to worry about a side dish, simply add some baby carrots and blanched-and-quartered potatoes to your freezer bag.

PREP DAY INGREDIENTS

2–3 pounds pork shoulder

Kosher salt and freshly ground black pepper, to taste

¼ cup honey

1 cup beef broth

½ cup balsamic vinegar

2 tablespoons Worcestershire sauce

1 teaspoon garlic powder

SERVING DAY INGREDIENTS

1 tablespoon cornstarch

1 tablespoon water

PREP DIRECTIONS

Rub the pork roast with salt and pepper and place it in a labeled 1-gallon freezer bag. In a medium bowl, combine the rest of the prep day ingredients. Add the mixture to the freezer bag, squeeze the remaining air out of the bag, and seal it. Lay the bag flat to freeze.

SERVING DAY DIRECTIONS

Allow the pork to thaw overnight in the refrigerator. On serving day, empty the contents of the freezer bag into the slow cooker, cover it, and cook on low for 8–10 hours. Remove the pork from the slow cooker. In a small bowl, mix together the cornstarch and water, then stir the mixture into the sauce in the slow cooker. Serve the roast topped with the thickened sauce.

Sweet Dijon Pork

Serves 6–8

Prep Time:
15 minutes

Cook Time:
8–10 hours

Cranberries, orange zest, and Dijon mustard transform a plain pork roast into a mouthwatering meal. Add a few quartered sweet potatoes to the freezer bag, and you have a lovely autumn-inspired dish that will bring the whole family to the table.

PREP DAY INGREDIENTS

3-4 pounds pork shoulder

Kosher salt and freshly ground black pepper, to taste

2 cups cranberries

½ cup brown sugar

1 tablespoon Dijon mustard

1 medium diced onion

½ teaspoon pumpkin pie spice

Zest of 1 orange

PREP DIRECTIONS

Rub the pork roast with salt and pepper and place it in a labeled 1-gallon freezer bag. In a medium bowl, combine the rest of the prep day ingredients. Add the mixture to the freezer bag, squeeze the remaining air out of the bag, and seal it. Lay the bag flat to freeze.

SERVING DAY DIRECTIONS

Allow the pork to thaw overnight in the refrigerator. On serving day, empty the contents of the freezer bag into the slow cooker, cover it, and cook on low for 8-10 hours.

Serves 4

Prep Time:
20 minutes

Cook Time:
8 hours

Twice-Spiced Louisiana-Style Ribs

These ribs are "Twice-Spiced" because you smother them in both dry seasoning and a spiced barbecue sauce. Letting them simmer and soak up the spices for 8 hours creates unbelievably tender and flavorful meat.

PREP DAY INGREDIENTS

1 rack baby back pork ribs

DRY RUB

1 tablespoon paprika

2 teaspoons salt

2 teaspoons garlic powder

1 teaspoon pepper

¾ teaspoon onion powder

¾ teaspoon dried leaf oregano

¾ teaspoon dried leaf thyme

½ teaspoon cayenne pepper

½ teaspoon Creole seasoning

¼ teaspoon crushed red pepper flakes

¼ cup packed brown sugar

BARBECUE SAUCE

1 cup barbecue sauce

½ teaspoon molasses

½ teaspoon Creole seasoning

¼ teaspoon garlic powder

⅛ teaspoon onion powder

SERVING DAY INGREDIENTS

½ cup water

PREP DIRECTIONS

Label a 1-gallon freezer bag. Place the ribs on a cutting board so that they curve up and away from the surface. Remove the silver skin and membrane. Slice the ribs into 4 even portions. Combine all of the dry rub ingredients in one small bowl and all of the barbecue sauce ingredients in another. Use your hands to rub the dry rub into both sides of the ribs. Spread half of the barbecue sauce over the ribs before placing them in the freezer bag. Squeeze the remaining air out of the bag and seal it. Lay the bag flat to freeze. Save the remaining barbecue sauce in a small freezer bag or freezer-safe container alongside the large freezer bag.

SERVING DAY DIRECTIONS

Allow the pork chops and extra sauce to thaw overnight in the refrigerator. On serving day, put the contents of the freezer bag and ½ cup water into the slow cooker, cover it, and cook on low for about 8 hours. Brush the ribs with the extra sauce before serving.

Boneless Barbecue Ribs

Barbecued ribs might be the best kind of summer comfort food. Serve them topped off with some fresh barbecue sauce and a side of cornbread or potato salad for a warm-weather feeling any night of the week.

PREP DAY INGREDIENTS

2-3 pounds boneless pork ribs

Kosher salt and freshly ground black pepper, to taste

½ large onion, thinly sliced

3 cloves garlic, minced

¼ cup brown sugar

½ cup apple sauce

1½ cups barbecue sauce

PREP DIRECTIONS

Rub the ribs with salt and pepper and place them in a labeled 1-gallon freezer bag with the onion. In a medium bowl, combine the rest of the ingredients. Add the mixture to the freezer bag, squeeze the remaining air out of the bag, and seal it. Lay the bag flat to freeze.

SERVING DAY DIRECTIONS

Allow the ribs to thaw completely in the refrigerator overnight. On serving day, empty the contents of the freezer bag into the slow cooker, cover it, and cook on low for 5-6 hours. Remove the ribs from the sauce and juices to serve.

Creamy Ranch Pork Chops

Serves 4-6

Prep Time:
5 minutes

Cook Time:
4-6 hours

With just three ingredients, this meal almost makes itself! Having trouble coming up with a side dish? Add some blanched-and-halved baby red potatoes to the freezer bag, then serve it all with your favorite steamed vegetable.

PREP DAY INGREDIENTS

4-6 boneless pork chops

2 (10.5-ounce) cans cream of chicken soup

1 envelope ranch dressing mix

PREP DIRECTIONS

Combine all ingredients in a large bowl. Label a 1-gallon freezer bag, place it in another large bowl, and pour in the mixture. Squeeze the remaining air out of the bag and seal it. Lay the bag flat to freeze.

SERVING DAY DIRECTIONS

Allow the pork chops to thaw overnight in the refrigerator. On serving day, pour the mixture into the slow cooker, cover it, and cook on low for 4-6 hours.

Crispy Pork Carnitas

Serves 6–8

Prep Time:
10 minutes

Cook Time:
6–8 hours

This shredded pork is tasty enough all on its own, but imagine it on a soft tortilla, topped with *queso fresco*, avocado, and a splash of lime juice. Yum! Broiling the shredded pork isn't necessary if you want to save time, but it gives the meat a nice caramelized texture.

PREP DAY INGREDIENTS

4-5 pounds pork shoulder, trimmed and cut into 3-inch chunks

1 cup beer, or equal parts chicken stock and apple cider vinegar

1 medium white onion, diced

4 cloves garlic, minced

1 tablespoon chipotle powder

2 teaspoons cumin

1 teaspoon black pepper

1 teaspoon chili powder

1½ teaspoons kosher salt

PREP DIRECTIONS

Combine all ingredients in a large bowl. Label a 1-gallon freezer bag, place it in another large bowl, and pour in the spiced pork mixture. Squeeze the remaining air out of the bag and seal it. Lay the bag flat to freeze.

SERVING DAY DIRECTIONS

Allow the pork to thaw overnight in the refrigerator. On serving day, pour the mixture into the slow cooker, cover it, and cook on low for 6-8 hours until the pork shreds easily using a fork. For crispy pork, move the shredded pork to two baking sheets lined with aluminum foil. Place them under the broiler until browned, about 5 minutes. Toss the browned pork in the juices in the slow cooker before serving.

Spiced Apple Pork

Once again, the sweetness of fruit brings out the best in pork while onions provide just enough bite to balance things out. Continue the theme with a side of baked sweet potatoes and a fresh veggie-packed salad topped with a fruit-based vinaigrette.

PREP DAY INGREDIENTS

2-2½ pounds boneless pork loin

1½ teaspoons kosher salt

½ teaspoon freshly ground black pepper

½ teaspoon ground cinnamon

2 large apples, peeled and sliced

½ medium onion, sliced

½ cup maple syrup

PREP DIRECTIONS

Label a 1-gallon freezer bag. Rub the pork loin with the salt, pepper, and cinnamon. Cut several slits into it to stuff with some of the apple slices, then place the whole thing in the freezer bag. In a large bowl, toss the sliced onion and the rest of the apples in the maple syrup, and pour the mixture into the freezer bag over the pork loin. Squeeze the remaining air out of the bag and seal it. Lay the bag flat to freeze.

SERVING DAY DIRECTIONS

Allow the pork to thaw overnight in the refrigerator. On serving day, pour the mixture into the slow cooker, cover it, and cook on low for about 8 hours.

Cranberry Pork Chops

Tart cranberries may seem like a fall staple, but their bright flavor works all year round. Of course, if you're looking for a meal to warm you up on a cool evening, baked sweet potatoes and cinnamon apples would be the perfect complement to these pork chops.

Serves 4-6

Prep Time: 15 minutes

Cook Time: 6–8 hours

PREP DAY INGREDIENTS

2 tablespoons unsalted butter

½ cup chopped onion

¼ cup chopped celery

1 clove garlic, minced

1 teaspoon kosher salt

4 boneless pork chops, about ½-inch thick

1 cup fresh or frozen cranberries

½ teaspoon dried thyme

¼ teaspoon freshly ground black pepper

2 tablespoons brown sugar

SERVING DAY INGREDIENTS

¼ cup chicken or vegetable broth

PREP DAY INGREDIENTS

Melt the butter in a large skillet over medium heat. Add the onion, celery, garlic, and salt and cook for 2-3 minutes. Set the mixture aside to cool. Sear the pork chops for 2 minutes on each side and set them aside. Once cool, combine the onion mixture and pork chops with the remaining prep day ingredients in a large bowl. Label a 1-gallon freezer bag, place it in another large bowl, and pour in the pork-chop mixture. Squeeze the remaining air out of the bag and seal it. Lay the bag flat to freeze.

SERVING DAY DIRECTIONS

Allow the pork chops to thaw overnight in the refrigerator. On serving day, pour ¼ cup broth and the contents of the freezer bag into the slow cooker, cover it, and cook on low for 6-8 hours.

Barbecue Pulled Pork

If you have hamburger buns and potato chips in your pantry and Barbecue Pulled Pork in your freezer, then you have a quick and satisfying meal your family will devour! Sure, you could just toss a pork shoulder and some barbecue sauce in your slow cooker, but the dry rub in this recipe will take your meal to the next level.

PREP DAY INGREDIENTS

2-2½ pounds pork shoulder

2 teaspoons kosher salt

1 teaspoon freshly ground black pepper

1 tablespoon paprika

2 cloves garlic, minced

½ medium onion, sliced

1 cup barbecue sauce

SERVING DAY INGREDIENTS

½ cup water

PREP DIRECTIONS

Label a 1-gallon freezer bag. Rub the pork shoulder with the salt, pepper, paprika, and garlic and place it in the freezer bag. Add the sliced onions to the bag. Pour the barbecue sauce over the pork in the bag. Squeeze the remaining air out of the bag and seal it. Lay the bag flat to freeze.

SERVING DAY DIRECTIONS

Allow the pork to thaw overnight in the refrigerator. On serving day, pour ½ cup water and the contents of the freezer bag into the slow cooker, cover it, and cook on low for 8-10 hours until the pork shreds easily using a fork. Shred the pork directly in the slow cooker or remove it, shred it, and return it to the slow cooker to toss in the sauce.

Maple-Bacon Pork Roast

Serves 6

Prep Time:
5 minutes

Cook Time:
7–8 hours

If you add bacon to anything, it's sure to be a hit. Maple Bacon Pork Roast is no exception! While roasted reds and steamed vegetables are great sides for this main dish, a little cornbread couldn't hurt.

PREP DAY INGREDIENTS

2-3 pounds boneless pork loin

4-5 strips uncooked bacon

½ cup maple syrup

3 tablespoons spicy brown mustard

2 tablespoons apple cider vinegar

1 tablespoon soy sauce

1½ teaspoons minced garlic

2 teaspoons freshly ground black pepper

PREP DIRECTIONS

Tightly wrap the pork loin with bacon to cover and place it in a labeled 1-gallon freezer bag. In a medium bowl, whisk together the remaining ingredients. Pour the mixture over the pork loin in the freezer bag. Squeeze the remaining air out of the bag and seal it. Lay the bag flat to freeze.

SERVING DAY DIRECTIONS

Allow the pork to thaw overnight in the refrigerator. On serving day, add the contents of the freezer bag to the slow cooker, cover it, and cook on low for 7-8 hours.

Homestyle Meatloaf

Imagine coming home at the end of a long day to a plateful of savory comfort food. Pair this easy make-ahead meatloaf with your favorite microwaveable vegetables for a simple dinner you don't have to think about. If you like your meatloaf saucy, finish it with a coating of ketchup or barbecue sauce.

PREP DAY INGREDIENTS

2 eggs, beaten

½ cup 2% milk

⅔ cup breadcrumbs

½ medium onion, chopped

1 teaspoon kosher salt

¼ teaspoon freshly ground black pepper

½ teaspoon sage

1½ pounds lean ground beef

PREP DIRECTIONS

Combine all ingredients in a large bowl, then form them into a loaf shape. Place the meatloaf in a labeled 1-gallon freezer bag, squeeze the remaining air out of the bag and seal it. Lay the bag flat to freeze.

SERVING DAY DIRECTIONS

Allow the meatloaf to thaw overnight in the refrigerator. Place it in the slow cooker and top it with as much ketchup or barbecue sauce as you like. On serving day, place the meatloaf in the slow cooker, cover it, and cook on low for 8-10 hours.

Sloppy Joes

Serves 6–8

Prep Time:
15 minutes

Cook Time:
2–3 hours

If you don't mind a little mess, Sloppy Joes are a great go-to meal for busy weeknights, post-game gatherings, and picnics alike. They'll put a smile on the face of even the pickiest eaters! For a slightly brighter flavor, dice up a good-sized green pepper and add it to the mix.

PREP DAY INGREDIENTS

1½ pounds ground beef

1 medium onion, finely chopped

2 cloves garlic, minced

½ cup chili sauce

1 (14-ounce) can tomato sauce

¼ cup water

1 tablespoon brown sugar

2 teaspoons Worcestershire sauce

2 teaspoons lemon juice

2 teaspoons chili powder

1 teaspoon dry mustard

Freshly ground black pepper, taste

SERVING DAY INGREDIENTS

6-8 rolls or hamburger buns

PREP DIRECTIONS

In a large pan, brown the beef over medium heat. Set it aside to drain and cool. Combine all prep day ingredients in a large bowl. Add the mixture to a labeled 1-gallon freezer bag, squeeze the remaining air out of the bag and seal it. Lay the bag flat to freeze.

SERVING DAY DIRECTIONS

Allow the beef to thaw overnight in the refrigerator. On serving day, pour the contents of the freezer bag into the slow cooker, cover it, and cook on low for 2–3 hours. Divide the mixture evenly among the hamburger buns.

Classic Spaghetti and Meatballs

Although you can leave the house and let this cook, you might want to stick around for this dish. The smell of simmering sauce is intoxicating! This recipe makes enough to feed a small army, so it's great for potlucks and parties. Make sure you keep some Parmesan cheese on the table for serving.

PREP DAY INGREDIENTS

Meatballs

1 cup seasoned bread crumbs

2 tablespoons grated Parmesan-Romano cheese

½ teaspoon kosher salt

1 teaspoon freshly ground black pepper

2 large eggs, lightly beaten

2 pounds ground beef

Sauce

1 large onion, finely chopped

1 medium green pepper, finely chopped

3 (15-ounce) cans tomato sauce

2 (14.5 ounce) cans diced tomatoes, undrained

1 (6-ounce) can tomato paste

6 cloves garlic, minced

2 dried bay leaves

1 teaspoon dried basil

1 teaspoon oregano

1 teaspoon parsley flakes

1 teaspoon kosher salt

½ teaspoon pepper

¼ teaspoon crushed red pepper flakes

SERVING DAY INGREDIENTS

2 pounds spaghetti noodles

PREP DIRECTIONS

Label a 1-gallon freezer bag. Combine the bread crumbs, cheese, salt, and pepper in a large bowl. Whisk in the eggs. Add in the beef and mix until well combined. Shape the mixture into meatballs, about 1½ inches in diameter. In a large skillet, brown the meatballs in batches over medium heat. In another large bowl, combine the sauce ingredients. Add the cooled meatballs to the freezer bag, then pour the sauce over them. Squeeze the remaining air out of the bag and seal it. Lay the bag flat to freeze.

SERVING DAY DIRECTIONS

Allow the meatballs to thaw overnight in the refrigerator. On serving day, pour the contents of the freezer bag into the slow cooker, cover it, and cook on low for 5–6 hours. Remove the bay leaves before serving. Cook the spaghetti according to the directions on the package and serve topped with the meatballs and sauce.

Pepper Steak

Serves 4

Prep Time:
15 minutes

Cook Time:
5 hours

When you think of Pepper Steak, you might imagine it served over rice at your favorite Asian restaurant. But this saucy dish is just as delicious on a hearty roll (especially if someone at your table turns up their nose at good take-out).

PREP DAY INGREDIENTS

1½ pounds top sirloin, cut into strips

1 large green bell pepper, sliced

1 large red bell pepper, sliced

½ medium white onion, sliced

½ cup water, divided

2 cubes beef bouillon

1 tablespoon cornstarch

3 tablespoon soy sauce

¼ teaspoon ground ginger

¼ teaspoon garlic powder

¼ teaspoon freshly ground black pepper

2 teaspoons brown sugar

SERVING DAY INGREDIENTS

4 rolls or hamburger buns

PREP DIRECTIONS

Add the steak, peppers, and onion to a labeled 1-gallon freezer bag. Add ¼ cup water and the bouillon cubes to a mug or microwave-safe container and microwave it for 60 seconds. Stir to dissolve the bouillon and set aside. Combine the rest of the ingredients (including the remaining ¼ cup water) in a large bowl until the cornstarch dissolves, add in the bouillon-water, and pour the whole mixture into the freezer bag. Squeeze the remaining air out of the bag and seal it. Lay the bag flat to freeze.

SERVING DAY DIRECTIONS

Allow the steak to thaw overnight in the refrigerator. On serving day, pour the contents of the freezer bag into the slow cooker, cover it, and cook on low for 5 hours. Divide the mixture evenly among the hamburger buns.

Ropa Vieja

Ropa Vieja is a classic Cuban dish so rich and flavorful you'll start craving it—which isn't a problem when you have this easy freezer meal available. Toss some cooked white rice with cilantro and a splash of lime juice for the perfect complement.

PREP DAY INGREDIENTS

1½ pounds of skirt steak or flank steak

1 teaspoon ground cumin

2 teaspoons oregano

1 teaspoon kosher salt

1 teaspoon freshly ground black pepper

3 cloves garlic, minced

1 medium onion, sliced

1 medium red bell pepper, sliced

½ cup water

2 cubes beef bouillon

1 (8-ounce) can tomato sauce

PREP DIRECTIONS

Rub the steak with the spices and garlic, then place it in a labeled 1-gallon freezer bag. Add the onion and pepper slices to the bag. Add ½ cup water and the bouillon cubes to a mug or microwave-safe container and microwave it for 60 seconds. Stir to dissolve the bouillon, then add the bouillon-water and tomato sauce to the bag. Squeeze the remaining air out of the bag and seal it. Lay the bag flat to freeze.

SERVING DAY DIRECTIONS

Allow the steak to thaw overnight in the refrigerator. On serving day, pour the contents of the freezer bag into the slow cooker, cover it, and cook on low for 8-10 hours. Move the steak to a cutting board, shred it, return it to the slow cooker, and toss it in the sauce before serving.

Mongolian Beef

If you think of steak as being tough, you haven't tried making it in the slow cooker. Mongolian Beef will melt in your mouth! Serve it over cooked white rice with a sprinkling of sliced green onion for a slow-simmered take on an Asian favorite.

Serves 4-6

Prep Time:
10 minutes

Cook Time:
4-5 hours

PREP DAY INGREDIENTS

1½ pounds flank steak

¼ cup cornstarch

2 tablespoons olive oil

½ teaspoon minced garlic

¾ cup soy sauce

¾ cup water

¾ cup brown sugar

1 cup grated carrot

PREP DIRECTIONS

Label a 1-gallon freezer bag. Slice the flank steak into strips about ¼-inch thick. Put the steak and the cornstarch into the freezer bag, seal the bag, and shake to coat the strips. Combine the rest of the ingredients in a large bowl, add the coated steak, and stir until the sauce coats the steak. Place the 1-gallon freezer bag in another large bowl and pour in the steak and sauce. Squeeze the remaining air out of the bag and seal it. Lay the bag flat to freeze.

SERVING DAY DIRECTIONS

Allow the steak to thaw overnight in the refrigerator. On serving day, add the contents of the bag to the slow cooker, cover it, and cook on low for 4-5 hours.

Honey-Balsamic Pot Roast

Traditional pot roast is a family favorite for a reason—slow-cooked chuck roast's hearty flavor and tenderness make it the perfect fuss-free comfort food. But with a little garlic, soy sauce, honey, and balsamic vinegar, this reimagined classic becomes fresh and exciting.

PREP DAY INGREDIENTS

2½-4 pounds chuck roast

½ cup honey

⅓ cup balsamic vinegar

2 cubes beef bouillon

1 tablespoon soy sauce

4 cloves garlic, minced

⅓ cup water

½ teaspoon kosher salt

PREP DIRECTIONS

Put the chuck roast into a labeled 1-gallon freezer bag. Combine the rest of the ingredients in a large bowl and then pour the mixture over the roast in the bag. Squeeze the remaining air out of the bag and seal it. Lay the bag flat to freeze.

SERVING DAY DIRECTIONS

Allow the roast to thaw overnight in the refrigerator. On serving day, pour the contents of the freezer bag into the slow cooker, cover it, and cook on low for 8-10 hours.

Brisket and Onions

Brisket is one of those cuts of meat made infinitely better by slow cooking it until it tenderizes and soaks up all the juices. In this recipe, caramelizing the onions and searing the meat add incredible flavor. And if you omit the soy sauce or use tamari instead, this main dish becomes gluten free!

Serves 6

Prep Time:
30 minutes

Cook Time:
6⅓–8⅓ hours

PREP DAY INGREDIENTS

1 tablespoon olive oil

2 large yellow or red onions, sliced into half moons

3½ pounds beef brisket

Kosher salt and freshly ground black pepper, to taste

6 cloves garlic, minced

2 cups beef broth

2 tablespoons Worcestershire sauce

1 tablespoon soy sauce

PREP DIRECTIONS

Label a 1-gallon freezer bag. Heat the olive oil in a large, deep pan over medium heat. Add the onions and sauté, stirring frequently, for about 20 minutes until lightly caramelized. Set the onions aside to cool. Season the brisket with salt and pepper and add it to the pan. Sear it on all sides over medium-high heat until browned and set it aside to cool. Once cool, place the brisket and onions in the freezer bag. Combine the garlic, broth, Worcestershire sauce, and soy sauce in a large bowl, and pour it into the bag over the brisket. Squeeze the remaining air out of the bag and seal it. Lay the bag flat to freeze.

SERVING DAY DIRECTIONS

Allow the brisket to thaw overnight in the refrigerator. On serving day, pour the contents of the freezer bag into the slow cooker, cover it, and cook on low for 6–8 hours until very tender. Remove the brisket and discard any excess fat before shredding it. Then return it to the slow cooker, stir it into the onions and sauce, and let it cook, covered, for another 15–20 minutes.

French Dip Roast Beef Sandwiches

These aren't ordinary sandwiches—spiced beef slowly simmers to tender perfection while the juices that fill the slow cooker become a rich sauce for dipping. You can add cold toppings, or for a special treat, top rolls with provolone cheese and toast them in the oven before adding the roast beef.

PREP DAY INGREDIENTS

1 tablespoon olive oil

chuck roast, trimmed of excess fat

uced-sodium soy sauce

ılar Coca-Cola

ınce) cans beef consommé or
1

on flakes

ıon beef bouillon powder

1 teaspoon garlic powder

½ teaspoon onion powder

½ teaspoon dried oregano

½ teaspoon salt

¼ teaspoon pepper

¼ teaspoon dried thyme

1 dried bay leaf

refrigerate dipping sauce to separate fat.

PREP DIRECTIONS

Label a 1-gallon freezer bag. Heat the olive oil in a large skillet over medium-high heat. Sear the roast on all sides until browned, then set it aside to cool. In the meantime, combine the rest of the ingredients in a large bowl. Put the roast into the freezer bag and pour the mixture in over it. Squeeze the remaining air out of the bag and seal it. Lay the bag flat to freeze.

SERVING DAY DIRECTIONS

Allow the roast to thaw overnight in the refrigerator. On serving day, pour the contents of the freezer bag into the slow cooker, cover it, and cook on low for 4 hours. Remove the roast to a cutting board and slice it across the grain as thinly as you like. Add the roast back into the slow cooker, re-cover, and continue cooking for 1–2 hours until tender. Remove the beef, discard the bay leaf, and strain the juices for serving as a dipping sauce.

Simple Stuffed Peppers

Serves 5

Prep Time:
10 minutes

Cook Time:
6 hours

The magic of Simple Stuffed Peppers is in how delicious they are using only five ingredients. But with so many varieties of salsa to choose from, you can add this recipe to your regular rotation without it ever getting stale. It's up to you whether you stuff the peppers on prep day and freeze them, or freeze the beef mixture and use fresh peppers on serving day. No need to brown the beef—just make sure it's cooked to the right temperature before serving (see the chart on page 4).

PREP DAY INGREDIENTS

1 pound lean ground beef

1 (15-ounce) jar salsa

1 cup cooked white or brown rice

1 cup shredded cheddar cheese

Kosher salt and freshly ground pepper, to taste

SERVING DAY INGREDIENTS

5 large bell peppers, any color

PREP DIRECTIONS

Combine all ingredients in a large bowl until well mixed. Place a labeled 1-gallon freezer bag in another large bowl and spoon in the beef mixture. Squeeze the remaining air out of the bag and seal it. Lay the bag flat to freeze.

SERVING DAY DIRECTIONS

Allow the beef mixture to thaw overnight in the refrigerator. On serving day, slice the tops off the peppers and remove their cores and seeds. Fill each pepper with a serving of the beef mixture, place them in the slow cooker, cover it, and cook on low for about 6 hours. If you prefer to serve the peppers with their tops, add them to the slow cooker before cooking.

Family-Favorite Pot Roast

Pot roast is one of those wonderful comfort foods that calls your name on a cold or challenging day. Why not let your slow cooker do the work so you can come home to that comfort? If you like a little more bite to your carrots, add them in about an hour before serving rather than packing them into the freezer bag.

PREP DAY INGREDIENTS

1 tablespoon olive oil

2 pounds chuck roast

Kosher salt and freshly ground pepper, to taste

2 cups sliced carrots

1 pound red potatoes, quartered

1 medium onion, sliced

1 clove garlic, minced

2 cups low-sodium beef broth

1 teaspoon dried thyme

PREP DIRECTIONS

Blanch the potatoes according to the directions on page 5. Heat the olive oil in a large pan over medium heat. Season the chuck roast with salt and pepper and sear it in the pan on all sides until browned. Allow the roast to cool before placing it in a labeled 1-gallon freezer bag. Add the rest of the ingredients to the bag, squeeze the remaining air out, and seal it. Lay the bag flat to freeze.

SERVING DAY DIRECTIONS

Allow the roast to thaw overnight in the refrigerator. On serving day, pour the contents of the freezer bag into the slow cooker, cover it, and cook on low for about 6 hours until tender.

Hearty Beef Lasagna

Homemade lasagna is a treat, but it's also a lot of work. Here, frozen meat sauce and a slow cooker turn it into a deliciously effortless meal.

Serves 7

Prep Time:
30 minutes

Cook Time:
4-5 hours

PREP DAY INGREDIENTS

½ pound ground beef

½ pound Italian sausage

1 large onion, chopped

1½ teaspoons kosher salt

½ teaspoon freshly ground black pepper

1 teaspoon Italian seasoning

2 tablespoons parsley

2 teaspoons garlic powder

2 tablespoons Worcestershire sauce

1 (6-ounce) can tomato paste

1 (29-ounce) can tomato sauce

2 tablespoons granulated sugar

1¼ cups water

SERVING DAY INGREDIENTS

4 cups shredded mozzarella cheese

1½ cups cottage cheese

½ cup grated Parmesan cheese

1 (8-ounce) package regular lasagna noodles, uncooked

Mozzarella cheese, for topping

PREP DAY DIRECTIONS

Label a 1-gallon freezer bag. In a large pan, brown the beef, sausage, and onion over medium heat. Add the rest of the prep day ingredients to the pan, stir, and simmer for 15-20 minutes. Allow the meat sauce to cool before placing it in the freezer bag. Squeeze the remaining air out of the freezer bag and seal it. Lay the bag flat to freeze.

SERVING DAY DIRECTIONS

Allow the meat sauce to thaw overnight in the refrigerator. On serving day, combine the cheeses in a large bowl. Add the meat sauce, noodles (breaking them to fit), and mixed cheese to the slow cooker to create three even layers, then top the last layer with more sauce and extra mozzarella. Cover and cook on low for 4-5 hours until the noodles are tender.

Maple Salmon with Shallots

While some cooking methods can dry salmon out, slow cooking ensures a moist, tender fillet. This recipe balances savory and sweet and erases the "fishy" taste that some picky eaters object to, making it a great weeknight dish for the whole family.

PREP DAY INGREDIENTS

6 (5-ounce) salmon fillets

1 tablespoon olive oil

½ cup sliced shallots

½ cup maple syrup

⅛ cup lime juice

¼ cup soy sauce

2 teaspoons crushed garlic

1 teaspoon minced ginger

PREP DIRECTIONS

Place the salmon fillets in a labeled 1-gallon freezer bag. Heat the olive oil in a small pan over medium heat. Add the shallots and allow them to cook until lightly caramelized, about 15 minutes. Combine them with the rest of the ingredients in a large bowl and pour the mixture into the bag over the salmon. Squeeze the remaining air out of the bag and seal it. Lay the bag flat to freeze.

SERVING DAY DIRECTIONS

Allow the salmon to thaw overnight in the refrigerator. On serving day, pour the contents of the freezer bag into the slow cooker, cover it, and let the salmon cook on high for 1 hour.

Asian-Style Salmon and Vegetables

While fish cooks much more quickly than chicken or beef, it can still benefit from a little time left to simmer in the slow cooker with flavorful ingredients. Whip up some brown rice on serving day to round out this healthy salmon dish.

PREP DAY INGREDIENTS

2 (5-ounce) salmon fillets

Kosher salt and freshly ground black pepper, to taste

1 (12- to 16-ounce) package frozen stir-fry vegetables

2 tablespoons soy sauce

2 tablespoons honey

2 tablespoons lemon juice

1 teaspoon sesame seeds

PREP DIRECTIONS

Label a 1-gallon freezer bag. Season the salmon fillets with salt and pepper and add them and the vegetables to the freezer bag. Combine the rest of the ingredients in a small bowl and pour the mixture into the bag. Squeeze the remaining air out of the freezer bag and seal it. Lay the bag flat to freeze.

SERVING DAY DIRECTIONS

Allow the salmon to thaw overnight in the refrigerator. On serving day, pour the contents of the freezer bag into the slow cooker, cover it, and cook on low for 2-3 hours. Serve the salmon and vegetables topped with a drizzle of the sauce.

Quick and Easy Barbecued Shrimp

Serves 4

Prep Time:
10 minutes

Cook Time:
1 hour

When you think of barbecue sauce, your mind might jump to chicken or pork. But the lightness of shrimp makes it a surprisingly perfect companion for the tangy topping. Serve Quick and Easy Barbecued Shrimp with a splash of lime juice and a side of cornbread on a warm, sunny day.

PREP DAY INGREDIENTS

2 pounds peeled and deveined shrimp, tails on

3 tablespoons unsalted butter

3 tablespoons Worcestershire sauce

2 teaspoons minced garlic

1 cup barbecue sauce

Kosher salt and freshly ground pepper, to taste

PREP DIRECTIONS

Combine all ingredients in a large bowl. Label a 1-gallon freezer bag, place it in another large bowl, and pour in the shrimp. Squeeze the remaining air out of the bag and seal it. Lay the bag flat to freeze.

SERVING DAY DIRECTIONS

Allow the shrimp to thaw overnight in the refrigerator. On serving day, pour the contents of the freezer bag into the slow cooker, cover it, and let the shrimp cook on low for 1 hour.

Buttery Shrimp Scampi

Serves 2-4

Prep Time:
10 minutes

Cook Time:
1½–2½ hours

Is there a more mouthwatering combination than lemon, butter, and garlic? Shrimp Scampi makes the most of all three ingredients! Top this bright dish with fresh parsley and serve it as an appetizer with crusty bread or as a main dish over cooked spaghetti.

PREP DAY INGREDIENTS

1 pound peeled and deveined shrimp, tails on

½ cup chicken broth

4 tablespoons olive oil

4 tablespoons unsalted butter

1 tablespoon minced garlic

Juice of 1 lemon

Kosher salt and freshly ground pepper, to taste

PREP DIRECTIONS

Combine all ingredients in a large bowl. Label a 1-gallon freezer bag, place it in another large bowl, and pour in the shrimp mixture. Squeeze the remaining air out of the bag and seal it. Lay the bag flat to freeze.

SERVING DAY DIRECTIONS

Allow the shrimp to thaw overnight in the refrigerator. On serving day, pour the contents of the freezer bag into the slow cooker, cover it, and let the shrimp cook on low for 1½–2½ hours.

Citrusy Fish Tacos

Filling your tacos with fresh fish is a great way to watch your waistline without forgoing your favorite dishes. And Citrusy Fish Tacos don't use breading or oil, making them even better for you than most. Finish them off with fresh toppings like avocado and lettuce— and maybe a little drizzle of sriracha mayonnaise.

PREP DAY INGREDIENTS

6 cod or tilapia fillets, frozen

1 (28-ounce) can diced tomatoes and green chiles, drained

½ teaspoon minced garlic

¼ cup chopped fresh cilantro

2 tablespoons lime juice

Kosher salt, to taste

SERVING DAY INGREDIENTS

Soft taco shells

PREP DIRECTIONS

Add the fish fillets to a labeled 1-gallon freezer bag. Combine the rest of the prep day ingredients in a large bowl and pour the mixture into the bag over the fillets. Squeeze the remaining air out of the bag and seal it. Lay the bag flat to freeze.

SERVING DAY DIRECTIONS

Allow the fish to thaw overnight in the refrigerator. On serving day, pour the contents of the freezer bag into the slow cooker, cover it, and let it cook on low for 4 hours. Shred the fish before serving in soft taco shells.

Mexican-Style Butternut Squash Quinoa

Serves 6-8

Prep Time:
10 minutes

Cook Time:
3-4 hours

This squash-based dish puts a spicy Mexican spin on the mild-mannered vegetable and pairs it with quinoa for a healthy meal you can feel good about putting on the table. Top it with any of your Taco Tuesday favorites, such as shredded cheddar cheese, fresh lime juice, sour cream, or chopped cilantro.

PREP DAY INGREDIENTS

4 cups peeled and cubed butternut squash

1 cup whole-kernel corn

1 (15.25-ounce) can black beans, drained and rinsed

1 cup uncooked quinoa, rinsed

1 teaspoon minced garlic

1 (14.5-ounce) can fire-roasted petite diced tomatoes, undrained

1 small jalapeño, diced (optional)

2 (19-ounce) cans mild red enchilada sauce

1 cup vegetable or chicken broth

1 packet taco seasoning

PREP DIRECTIONS

Combine all ingredients in a large bowl. Label a 1-gallon freezer bag, place it in another large bowl, and pour in the quinoa mixture. Squeeze the remaining air out of the bag and seal it. Lay the bag flat to freeze.

SERVING DAY DIRECTIONS

Allow the quinoa mixture to thaw overnight in the refrigerator. On serving day, pour the contents of the freezer bag into the slow cooker, cover it, and let it cook on high for 3-4 hours until the quinoa is cooked and the squash is tender.

Desserts

Apple-Cinnamon Crumble

The smell of apples and cinnamon filling the house is sure to help you relax at the end of the day. But the best part about this dessert is that it tastes much richer than it is, which means it won't keep you up at night.

PREP DAY INGREDIENTS

2 Granny Smith apples

1 cup granola

⅛ cup maple syrup

¼ cup apple juice

2 tablespoons unsalted butter

1 teaspoon ground cinnamon

½ teaspoon ground nutmeg

PREP DIRECTIONS

Peel and core the apples, then cut them into chunks or slices. In a large bowl, combine the rest of the ingredients and then stir in the apples. Label a 1-gallon freezer bag, place it in another large bowl, and pour in the mixture. Squeeze the remaining air out of the bag and seal it. Lay the bag flat to freeze.

SERVING DAY DIRECTIONS

On serving day, pour the contents of the freezer bag into the slow cooker, cover it, and cook on low for 4 hours.

Blueberry Crumble

Serves 4-6

Prep Time:
10 minutes

Cook Time:
3-5 hours

Did you know that you can use baking dishes in your slow cooker? If you don't mind missing some of your dishes for a while, you can freeze individual portions right in ramekins, then pop them into the slow cooker on serving day. This ensures a better presentation when you want your desserts to impress. And if impressing is the goal, top this crumble with fresh blueberries, chopped almonds, and some fresh mint.

PREP DAY INGREDIENTS

16 ounces frozen blueberries

1 cup quick oats

½ cup pecan pieces

½ cup almond meal

½ teaspoon salt

¼ cup honey

5 tablespoons unsalted butter, softened

PREP DIRECTIONS

Combine the oats, pecans, and almond meal in a large bowl. Add the honey and butter and mix with a fork to create a crumbly texture. Label a 1-gallon freezer bag, place it in another large bowl, and pour in the crumble mixture. Next, add the blueberries to the bag. (When you pour the mixture out, the berries will be on the bottom of the slow cooker and the crumble on the top.) Squeeze the remaining air out of the bag and seal it. Lay the bag flat to freeze.

SERVING DAY DIRECTIONS

On serving day, pour the contents of the freezer bag into the slow cooker so that they're spread over the bottom. (It doesn't have to be layered perfectly—some mixing is fine.) Cover the slow cooker and cook on low for 3-5 hours.

"Baked" Cinnamon Apples

Cinnamon and melted butter transform this healthy snack into a decadent dessert. Everyone has a favorite variety of apple, and this recipe turns out amazing no matter which you use, so use whichever kind you like best! For a prettier presentation, you can core the apples and slice them horizontally in rings.

PREP DAY INGREDIENTS

6-8 medium apples

1 stick unsalted butter, melted

½ brown sugar

½ teaspoon ground cinnamon

¼ teaspoon ground nutmeg

⅛ teaspoon kosher salt

1 teaspoon orange zest

½ cup chopped walnuts

PREP DIRECTIONS

Core and slice the apples. In a large bowl, combine the rest of the ingredients and then stir in the apples. Label a 1-gallon freezer bag, place it in another large bowl, and pour in the mixture. Squeeze the remaining air out of the bag and seal it. Lay the bag flat to freeze.

SERVING DAY DIRECTIONS

On serving day, pour the contents of the freezer bag into the slow cooker, cover it, and cook on high for 2½ hours until the apples are tender.

Plum Compote

Serves 6

Prep Time:
10 minutes

Cook Time:
3 hours

Sometimes the simplest recipes are the best—honey, vanilla, and cinnamon complement the plums rather than overpowering them. Pour this warm fruit over cheesecake or vanilla ice cream for a treat that lets it shine. If you prefer mixed fruit, substitute diced apples and pears for a few of the plums.

PREP DAY INGREDIENTS

9 plums, pitted and quartered

¼ cup honey

½ teaspoon vanilla extract

½ teaspoon ground cinnamon

PREP DIRECTIONS

Combine all ingredients in a large bowl. Label a 1-gallon freezer bag, place it in another large bowl, and pour in the mixture. Squeeze the remaining air out of the bag and seal it. Lay the bag flat to freeze.

SERVING DAY DIRECTIONS

On serving day, pour the contents of the freezer bag into the slow cooker, cover it, and cook on low for 3 hours until the plums are tender.

Red Velvet Cupcakes

Did you know that you can make cake in your slow cooker? You can pour the batter directly into the insert, pour it into a cake pan or baking dish that fits inside, or even pour it into cupcake liners. And these soft and scrumptious Red Velvet Cupcakes couldn't be easier—just add pudding mix to your favorite boxed cake mix brand.

PREP DAY INGREDIENTS

1 (15.25-ounce) box red velvet cake mix

1 (3.4-ounce) package chocolate instant pudding mix

1¼ cups 2% milk

½ cup vegetable oil

3 large eggs

SERVING DAY INGREDIENTS

1 (16-ounce) can cream cheese frosting

PREP DIRECTIONS

Combine all prep day ingredients in a large bowl. Label a 1-gallon freezer bag, place it in another large bowl, and pour in the cupcake batter. Squeeze the remaining air out of the bag and seal it. Lay the bag flat to freeze.

SERVING DAY DIRECTIONS

Allow the batter to thaw overnight in the refrigerator. On serving day, place 12 paper cupcake liners in your slow cooker and divide the batter evenly among them. Cover the slow cooker and cook on low for 3½ hours or until a toothpick inserted into the center of a cupcake comes out clean. Allow the cupcakes to cool for up to 30 minutes before topping them with the cream cheese frosting.

Serves 10–12

Prep Time:
15 minutes

Cook Time:
2–3 hours

Strawberry Shortcake

The simplicity of shortcake makes it a great base not just for strawberries, but for whatever fruit combination you like. Add some blueberries and raspberries, or go tropical with mango and pineapple! If a larger loaf pan won't fit into your slow cooker, use whatever size you need, such as multiple mini pans.

PREP DAY INGREDIENTS

2 tablespoons unsalted butter, melted

1 cup sugar

2 large eggs

2½ cups flour

½ teaspoon salt

2 teaspoons baking powder

1 cup 2% milk

1 teaspoon vanilla

SERVING DAY INGREDIENTS

1 pound strawberries, de-stemmed and sliced

1 can or tub whipped cream

PREP DIRECTIONS

Combine the butter, sugar, and eggs in a large bowl. Add the flour, salt, and baking powder and mix until crumbly. Stir in the milk and vanilla until the batter is mostly smooth. Label a 1-gallon freezer bag, place it in another large bowl, and pour in the cake batter. Squeeze the remaining air out of the bag and seal it. Lay the bag flat to freeze.

SERVING DAY DIRECTIONS

Allow the batter to thaw overnight in the refrigerator. On serving day, pour it into an 8.5" x 4.5" x 2.75" loaf pan and cover it with greased foil. Place the loaf pan in the slow cooker, cover it, and cook on low for 2–3 hours or until a toothpick inserted into the center comes out clean. Allow the cake to cool for up to 30 minutes before serving, and top with strawberries and whipped cream.

White Chocolate Cake with Raspberries

Serves 10

Prep Time:
10 minutes

Cook Time:
3½ hours

White chocolate and raspberries were made for each other and are only made better when folded into a deliciously moist white cake. It's up to you whether you want to top this with frosting or just powdered sugar (and maybe some fresh raspberries or a drizzle of raspberry syrup). Any way you slice it, this is a quick and easy dessert your guests are sure to adore!

PREP DAY INGREDIENTS

1 (15.25-ounce) box white cake mix

1 (3.4-ounce) package white chocolate instant pudding mix

1¼ cups milk

½ cup vegetable oil

3 large eggs

½ cup white chocolate chips

1½ cups frozen raspberries

PREP DIRECTIONS

Combine all ingredients in a large bowl. Label a 1-gallon freezer bag, place it in another large bowl, and pour in the cake batter. Squeeze the remaining air out of the bag and seal it. Lay the bag flat to freeze.

SERVING DAY DIRECTIONS

Allow the batter to thaw overnight in the refrigerator. On serving day, pour the batter into the slow cooker, cover it, and cook on low for 3½ hours or until a toothpick inserted into the center comes out clean.

Simply Delicious Brownies

Serves 8

Prep Time:
10 minutes

Cook Time:
2½ hours

Whoever invented the fudgy, chocolatey dessert we call brownies deserves an award. Top these beauties with vanilla bean ice cream and chopped nuts to bring out their best. Here's a little tip for you: the trick to a cleanly sliced brownie is to use a plastic or silicone knife, which tugs less on the brownies as it cuts them.

PREP DAY INGREDIENTS

12 tablespoons unsalted butter, melted

1½ cups granulated sugar

½ teaspoon kosher salt

3 large eggs

1 cup unsweetened cocoa powder

1 cup all-purpose flour

½ cup dark chocolate chips

½ cup chopped walnuts (optional)

PREP DIRECTIONS

Combine the butter, sugar, salt, and eggs in a large bowl. Fold in the cocoa powder and flour until well mixed. Label a 1-gallon freezer bag, place it in another large bowl, and pour in the batter. Squeeze the remaining air out of the bag and seal it. Lay the bag flat to freeze.

SERVING DAY DIRECTIONS

Allow the batter to thaw overnight in the refrigerator. On serving day, pour the batter into the slow cooker, cover it, and cook on low for 2½ hours or until a toothpick inserted into the center comes out clean. Allow the brownies to cool before slicing them.

Mixed-Berry Cobbler

Mixed-Berry Cobbler is an amazing way to make the most of fresh (or frozen) strawberries, blackberries, blueberries, and raspberries. Choose a couple of your favorites, or add them all in! You can't go wrong with this super simple slow-simmered recipe.

PREP DAY INGREDIENTS

1 (15.25-ounce) box vanilla cake mix

8 tablespoons unsalted butter, melted

3 tablespoons granulated sugar

3 cups fresh or frozen mixed berries

PREP DIRECTIONS

Combine the cake mix, butter, and sugar in a large bowl until crumbly. Label a 1-gallon freezer bag, place it in another large bowl, and pour in the crumble mixture. Next, add the berries to the bag. (When you pour the mixture out, the berries will be on the bottom of the slow cooker and the crumble on the top.) Squeeze the remaining air out of the bag and seal it. Lay the bag flat to freeze.

SERVING DAY DIRECTIONS

On serving day, pour the contents of the freezer bag into the slow cooker so that they're spread over the bottom. (It doesn't have to be layered perfectly—mixing is fine.) Cover the slow cooker and cook on low for 3½ hours.

Lemon Poppy Seed Cake

This light and sunny cake is perfect for eating outside on a warm summer day. Keep things simple by topping it with a dusting of powdered sugar, or mix together 1 cup powdered sugar and 1–2 tablespoons lemon juice for a citrusy-sweet glaze.

PREP DAY INGREDIENTS

1 (15.25-ounce) box yellow cake mix

1 (3.4-ounce) package lemon instant pudding mix

1¼ cups water

½ cup vegetable oil

3 large eggs

1 teaspoon vanilla extract

2 tablespoons poppy seeds

PREP DIRECTIONS

Combine all ingredients in a large bowl. Label a 1-gallon freezer bag, place it in another large bowl, and pour in the cake batter. Squeeze the remaining air out of the bag and seal it. Lay the bag flat to freeze.

SERVING DAY DIRECTIONS

Allow the batter to thaw overnight in the refrigerator. On serving day, pour the batter into the slow cooker, cover it, and cook on low for 3½ hours or until a toothpick inserted into the center comes out clean.

Index

ELLA SANDERS is a comfort food enthusiast who loves spending time at the table with friends and family. She shares her enthusiasm for cooking with anyone who's interested and specializes in making traditional meals with unexpected flavor and flair. Ella lives with her husband and two boys in Portland, Maine.

LOOK FOR THESE OTHER COOKBOOKS BY
ELLA SANDERS!

SUPER FAST INSTANT POT PRESSURE COOKER COOKBOOK
100 EASY RECIPES FOR EVERY MULTI-COOKER
HEATHER RODINO & ELLA SANDERS

THE BEST **AIR FRYER RECIPES ON THE PLANET**
OVER 125 EASY, FOOLPROOF FRIED FAVORITES WITHOUT ALL THE FAT
GREAT RESULTS FOR EVERY AIR FRYER!
ELLA SANDERS

COPPER Magic!
NO-FAIL RECIPES FOR THE Revolutionary New Nonstick Cookware
ELLA SANDERS

COPPER Magic! ONE-POT MEALS
NO-FUSS RECIPES FOR THE REVOLUTIONARY NEW NONSTICK COOKWARE
ELLA SANDERS
Author of THE ULTIMATE INSTANT POT COOKBOOK

BRAND-NEW, GO-TO RECIPES FOR EVERY MULTI-COOKER!
Easy-Freeze INSTANT POT PRESSURE COOKER COOKBOOK
100 Freeze-Ahead, Make-in-Minutes Recipes
ELLA SANDERS
Best-selling author of The Ultimate Instant Pot Pressure Cooker Cookbook

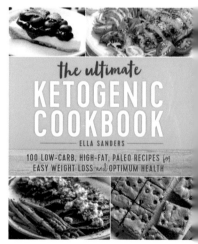

the ultimate **KETOGENIC COOKBOOK**
ELLA SANDERS
100 LOW-CARB, HIGH-FAT, PALEO RECIPES for EASY WEIGHT LOSS and OPTIMUM HEALTH